Microprocessors in Space

Patrick H. Stakem

4th edition

Table of Contents

Introduction

This book discusses the use of microprocessors in space missions, from the earliest 4-bit machines to the most current 64-bit implementations. We have seen the transition from monolithic processors with extensive glue logic, to IP cores instantiated in FPGA's. This discussion is not all-inclusive, but gives the high-lights of the microprocessors sent and being sent into space, and the problems of supplying and sustaining their operations there. Microprocessors orbit the earth, sit on other planets, and have left the Solar system into interstellar space. They are the key components for spacecraft autonomy, and for collecting, storing, and returning the volumes of information that we receive from off-planet sources. The basis technology for microprocessors and their associated memory and communications follows exponential growth curves in capability, referred to as "Moore's Law." Space-based electronics necessarily lags the Earth-based state-of-the-art by several generations, due to the need to address the harsh operating conditions. Spacecraft microprocessors are a special subset of embedded computers. Most spacecraft include 10's of processors, doing tasks such as attitude and orbit control, power monitoring and control, telemetry formatting and command handling, data storage management, and instrument control. Without these microprocessors, the amount that we know about our sun, neighboring planets, and the intervening space would be vastly limited.

Early flight computers were custom designs, but cost and performance issues have driven the development of variants of commercial chips. Aerospace applications are usually classic embedded applications. Space applications are rather limited in number, and, until recently, almost exclusively meant National Aeronautics and Space Administration (NASA), European Space Association (ESA), National AeroSpace Development Agency (NASDA) - Japan, or some other government agency. Flight systems electronics usually require MIL-STD-883b, Class-S, radiation-hard (total dose), SEU-tolerant parts. MIL-STD-883 is the standard for testing and screening of parts. Specific issues of radiation tolerance are discussed in MIL-M-38510. Class-S parts are specifically for space-flight use. Because of the need for qualifying the parts for space, the state-of-the-art in spaceborne electronics usually lags that of the equivalent terrestrial commercial parts by 5 years. The initial crewed spacecraft, the Mercury capsule, didn't have a computer. The second model, the Gemini, had a flight computer constructed of discrete chips, using resistor-transistor logic

The advantage of a radiation-hard version of a commercial chipset is the ability to piggyback onto the existing set of software tools, applications, and development environments, as well as a pool of software developers.

Processors used in aerospace applications, as any semiconductor-based electronics, need to meet stringent selection, screening, packaging and testing requirements, and characterizations because of the unique environment. Most aerospace electronics, and the whole understanding of radiation effects, were driven by the cold war defense buildup from the 1960's through the 1980's. This era was characterized by the function-at-any-cost, melt-before-fail design philosophy. In the 1990, the byword was COTS -- use of Commercial, Off-The-Shelf products. Thus, instead of custom, proprietary processor architecture's, we are now seeing the production of specialized products derived from commercial lines. In the era of decreasing markets, the cost of entry, and of maintaining presence in this tiny market niche, are prohibitively high for many companies.

FPGA -based solutions are now mainstream for spacecraft computing usage, using hard or soft-cores of standard microprocessor architectures. Either the entire structure is constructed to be radiation-hard, or triplication with selected hardened circuits is applied.

Forward to the Second Edition.

This book is the 4th in a Space series. It has been updated, revised, expanded and re-edited, with new material being added. A glossary is included. Updates on the latest RISC-V architectures are discussed

Author

The author built his first home computer in 1976 or so, a 16-bit TI-9900 design. He built and got working an Altair 8800 for work in 1975. He went to the Big Computer Faire in Atlantic City, and saw two guys, both named Steve, from California, with a wooden-cased project that probably wasn't going to go anywhere commercially. His Aerospace career has revolved around support for space-based microprocessors and computers for NASA since 1971. In that year, he discovered that computers were included in satellites.

Mr. Stakem received a Bachelor's Degree in Electrical Engineering from Carnegie Mellon University, and masters in Physics and Computer Science from the Johns Hopkins University. He has followed a career as a NASA support contractor since 1971, working at every NASA Site. He is associated with the Graduate Computer Science Department at Loyola University in Maryland, and the Whiting School of Engineering of the Johns Hopkins University, as well as Capitol Technology University.

The Challenges of the Space Environment

This section discusses the major environmental obstacles to the use of sophisticated electronics in space, and the mitigation techniques that can be applied.

Radiation

"The Valkyrior are warlike virgins, mounted upon horses and armed with helmets and spears. /.../ When they ride forth on their errand, their armour sheds a strange flickering light, which flashes up over the northern skies, making what men call the "aurora borealis", or "Northern Lights"." Thomas Bulfinch, 1855.

Well, that's one theory. Here on the surface of the planet, we are mostly shielded by the atmosphere and by the magnetic field lines (but only against charged particles) from the fury of the Sun. In space, or on other planetary surfaces, the situation is much different.

There are two radiation problem areas: cumulative dose, and single event. Operating above the Van Allen belts of particles trapped in Earth's magnetic flux lines, spacecraft are exposed to the full fury of the Universe. Earth's magnetic poles do not align with the rotational poles, so the inner Van Allen belts dip to around 200 kilometers in the South Atlantic, leaving a region called the South Atlantic Anomaly. The magnetic field lines are good at deflecting charged particles, but mostly useless against electromagnetic radiation and uncharged particles such as neutrons. One trip across the Van Allen belts can ruin a spacecraft's electronics. Some spacecraft turn off sensitive electronics for several minutes every ninety minutes – every pass through the low dipping belts in the South Atlantic.

The Earth and other planets are constantly immersed in the solar wind, a flow of hot plasma emitted by the Sun in all directions, a result of the two-million-degree heat of the Sun's outermost layer, the Corona. The solar wind usually reaches Earth with a velocity around 400 km/s, with a density around 5 ions/cm^3. During magnetic storms on the Sun, flows can be several times faster, and stronger. The Sun tends to have an eleven year cycle of maxima. A solar flare is a large explosion in the Sun's atmosphere that can release as much as 6×10^{25} joules in one event, equal to about one sixth of the Sun's total energy output every second. Solar flares are frequently coincident with sun spots. Solar flares, being releases of large amounts of energy, can trigger Coronal Mass Ejections, and accelerate lighter particles to near the speed of light.

The size of the Van Allen Belts shrink and expand in response to the Solar Wind. The wind is made up of particles, electrons up to 10 Million electron volts (MeV), and protons up to 100 Mev – all ionizing doses. One charged particle can knock thousands of electrons loose from the semiconductor lattice, causing noise, spikes, and current surges. Since memory elements are capacitors, they can be damaged or discharged, essentially changing state.

Vacuum tube based technology is essentially immune from radiation effects.

Not that just current electronics are vulnerable. The Great Auroral Exhibition of 1859 interacted with the then-extant telegraph lines acting as antennae, such that batteries were not needed for the telegraph apparatus to operate for hours at a time. Some telegraph systems were set on fire. The whole show is referred to as the Carrington Event, after British Scientist Richard Carrington.

Around other planets, the closer we get to the Sun, the bigger the impact of solar generated particles, and the less predictable they are. Auroras have been observed on Venus, in spite of the planet not having an observed magnetic field. The impact of the solar particles becomes less of a problem with the outer planets. Auroras have also been observed on Mars, and the magnetic filed of Jupiter, Saturn, and some of the moons cause their "Van Allen belts" to trap large numbers of energetic particles, which cause more problems for spacecraft in transit. Both Jupiter and Saturn have magnetic field greater than Earth's. Not all planets have a magnetic field, so not all get charged particle belts.

Radiation Hardness Issues for Space Flight Applications

A complete discussion of the physics of radiation damage to semiconductors is beyond the scope of this document. However, an overview of the subject is presented. The tolerance of semiconductor devices to radiation must be examined in the light of their damage susceptibility. The problems fall into two broad categories, those caused by cumulative dose, and those transient events caused by asynchronous very energetic particles, such as those experienced during a period of intense solar flare activity. The unit of absorbed dose of radiation is the rad, representing the absorption of 100 ergs of energy per gram of material. A kilo-rad is one thousand rads. At 10k rad, death in humans is almost instantaneous. One hundred kilo-rad is typical in the vicinity of Jupiter's radiation belts. Ten to twenty kilo-rad is typical for spacecraft in low Earth orbit, but the number depends on how much time the spacecraft spends outside the Van Allen belts, which act as a shield by trapping energetic particles.

Absorbed radiation can cause temporary or permanent changes in the material. Usually, neutrons, being uncharged, do minimal damage, but energetic protons and electrons cause lattice or ionization damage in the material, and resultant parametric changes. For example, the leakage current can increase, or bit states can change. Certain technologies and manufacturing processes are known to produce devices that are less susceptible to damage than others.

Radiation tolerance of 100 kilo-rad is usually more than adequate for low Earth orbit (LEO) missions that spend most of their life below the shielding of the Van Allen belts. For Polar missions, a higher total dose is expected, from 100k to 1 mega-rad per year.

For synchronous, equatorial orbits, that are used by many communication satellites, and some weather satellites, the expected dose is several kilo-rad per year. Finally, for planetary missions to Venus, Mars, Jupiter, Saturn, and beyond, requirements that are even more stringent must be met. For one thing, the missions usually are unique, and the cost of failure is high. For missions towards the sun, the higher fluence of solar radiation must be taken into account. The larger outer planets, such as Jupiter and Saturn, have large radiation belts around them as well.

Cumulative radiation dose causes a charge trapping in the oxide layers, which manifests as a parametric change in the devices. Total dose effects may be a function of the dose rate, and annealing of the device may occur, especially at elevated temperatures. Annealing refers to the self-healing of radiation induced defects. This can take minutes to months, and is not applicable for lattice damage. The total dose susceptibility of the Transputer has been measured at 35-50 k-rad with no internal memory. The internal memory or registers are the most susceptible area of the chip, and is usually deactivated for operations in a radiation environment. The gross indication of radiation damage is the increased power consumption of the device, and one researcher reported a doubling of the power consumption at failure. In addition, failed devices could operate at a lower clock rate, leading to speculation that a key timing parameter was being effected in this case.

Single event upsets (seu's) are the response of the device to direct high energy isotropic flux, such as cosmic rays, or the secondary effects of high energy particles colliding with other matter (such as shielding). Large transient currents may result, causing changes in logic state (bit flips), unforeseen operation, device latch-up, or burnout. The transient currents can be monitored as an indicator of the onset of SEU problems. After SEU, the results on the operation of the processor are somewhat unpredictable. Mitigation of problems caused by SEU's involves self-test, memory scrubbing, and forced resets.

The LET (linear energy transfer) is a measure of the incoming particles' delivery of ionizing energy to the device. Latch-up refers to the inadvertent operation of a parasitic SCR (silicon control rectifier), triggered by ionizing radiation. In the area of latch-up, the chip can be made inherently hard due to use of the Epitaxial process for fabrication of the base layer. Even the use of an Epitaxial layer does not guarantee complete freedom from latch-up, however. The next step generally involves a silicon on insulator (SOI) or Silicon on Sapphire (SOS) approach, where the substrate is totally insulated, and latch-ups are not possible.

In some cases, shielding is effective, because even a few millimeters of aluminum can stop electrons and protons. However, with highly energetic or massive particles (such as alpha particles, helium nuclei), shielding can be counter-productive. When the atoms in the shielding are hit by an energetic particle, a cascade of lower energy, lower mass particles results. These can cause as much or more damage than the original source particle.

Mitigation Techniques

The effects of radiation on silicon circuits can be mitigated by redundancy, the use of specifically radiation hardened parts, Error Detection and Correction (EDAC) circuitry, and scrubbing techniques. Hardened chips are produced on special insulating substrates such as Sapphire. Bipolar technology chips can withstand radiation better than CMOS technology chips, at the cost of greatly increased power consumption. Shielding techniques are also applied. In error detection and correction techniques, special encoding of the stored information provides a protection against flipped bits, at the cost of additional bits to store. Redundancy can also be applied at the device or box level, with the popular Triple Modular Redundancy (TMR) technique triplicating everything, and based on the assumption that the probability of a double failure is less than that of a single failure. Watchdog timers are used to reset systems unless they are themselves reset by the software. Of course, the watchdog timer circuitry is also susceptible to failure.

Thermal issues

Radiation is not the only problem. In space, things are either too hot or too cold. On the inner planets toward the Sun, things are too hot. On the planets outward of Earth, things are too cold. In space, there is no gravity, so there are no conduction currents. Cooling is by conduction and radiation only. This requires heat-generating electronics to have a conductive path to a radiator. That makes board design for chips, and chip packaging, complex and expensive.

Mechanical issues

In zero gravity, every thing floats, whether you want it to or not. Floating conductive particles, bits of solder or bonding wire, can short out circuitry. This is mitigated by conformal coatings, but the perimeter of the chip die is usually ground, and cannot be coated due to manufacturing sequences.

The challenges of electronics in space are daunting, but much is now understood about the failure mechanisms, and techniques to address them.

Computer Architecture

Generally, a computer has one (or more) central processing units, memory, and input/output functionality. When microprocessors where fist introduced, the chip contained only the cpu. Memory and I/O were provided by separate chips. Now, the state of the art allows memory and I/O to be combined on the same chip (microcontroller), and even multiple cpus on one chip (Multicore).

Central Processing Unit

A *cpu* performs arithmetic and logic functions on data, and provides flow of control. The arithmetic functions we would like to have performed are additional, subtraction, multiplication, and division. The logical operations on binary data include inversion, AND, OR, Exclusive OR, and derivative functions such as Negated-AND (NAND), Negated-OR (NOR), and Negated-Exclusive OR (NXOR). The cpu is responsible for fetching instructions and data from memory. Specialized units such as a floating point unit (FPU) or a graphics processing unit (GPU) operate on data in a different format. A cpu is general purpose, and the FPU and GPU, as well as Digital Signal Processors (DSP) are specialized, optimized to particular processing needs.

Microcontrollers

A microcontroller is a simple CPU plus some memory and input-output. The idea is to have a single-chip solution to minimize costs. Microcontrollers are not used as general number crunchers, but in dedicated control applications such as elevators, gas pumps, and cell phones.

Where the modern CPU would include several levels of cache memory and multiple computer cores because the fabrication technology would support that level of complexity, a microcontroller would contain the cpu (s) memory, and I/O to support a single chip solution. This simplifies the rest of the system design, and reduces the parts count, which leads to lower costs.

Digital Signal Processors

A Digital Signal Processor (DSP) is similar to a general purpose CPU, but provides specialized operations for DSP-type operations on specialized data formats. Originally, the DSP function would be implemented by software running in a general purpose CPU. DSP operations usually have time deadline constraints (hard real time requirements), and the throughput of the CPU is limited. DSP for audio evolved from sonar processing, and video data processing evolved from radar.

DSP's operate on multimedia data types, and include special-purpose operations derived from the digital signal processing realm. This includes the Multiply-and-Accumulate (mac), a digital filtering primitive. Two of the DSP-specific units that have been used on spacecraft include the Motorola 56000 and TI's TMS320C40.

Flight Microprocessor Usage
This is not by any means a comprehensive list.

Mission	cpu
Cassini	1750A
Clementine	1750A, 32-bit RISC
Cluster (ESA)	1750a
Coriolis	RAD6000
Cubesat	8051,PIC, Arduino
Deep Impact	RadLite 750
Deep Space-1	RAD6000
EO-1/Warp	Mongoose V
EOS Aqua	1750A (4) and 8051 (2)
EOS Aura	1750A (4) and 8051 (2)
ESO Terra	1750A (2)

14

EUVE	1750A
FAST	8085 (2)
FUSE	80386, 80387, 68000
Galileo	2900 (2) 1802 (19)
Galileo AACS	ATAC (bit slice)
Gravity Probe B	RAD6000
GRO	9900, LSI-11
HealthSat-II	80C186(2), 80C188
HESSI	RAD6000
HETE-2	M56001(DSP) (8), Transputer
HST	80386, 80486
Icesat, GLAS	Mongoose V
ICM	R3000
ISEE	8080
ISS	i80386, Pentium
Landsat-D	8x300, 8x305
Mangalyaan (Mars)	MA31750 (1750A)
MAP	Mongoose V, UTMC 69R000
Mars98	Rad 6000
Mars Climate Orbiter	RAD6000
Mars Observer	1759A
Mars Pathfinder	RAD6000
Mars Pathfinder Rover	80C85
Mars Polar lander	RAD6000
Mars Surveyor	1750A
Messenger-Mercury	RAD6000 (2)
Mighty Sat-II	TMS320C40 (DSP) (4)
MSTI-1,2	1750A
MSTI-3	1750A, R3000
New Horizons (Pluto)	Mongoose-V (4)
Pluto Express	32-bit RISC

PoSat-1	80c186, TMS320C25 and C30
Rosetta (ESA)	1750A
Sampex	80386, 80387
SIRTF	RAD6000
SMEX	80386, 80387
SMEX-lite	RAD6000
SMM	6100A
Snap-1	StrongARM
Stardust	RAD6000
TDRSS, early	2901
Tiros, Block 5D	F-8

4-bit Processors

Before the 8-bit processors came the 4-bit processors. Actually, 4-bits makes some sense – it can handle the binary coded decimal (BDC) numbers, 10 digits contained in a 4-bit word, with 6 symbols left over. Early examples of the 4-bit processors were the Intel 4004 and 4040. The 4004 is generally considered the world's first commercially available microprocessor. Intel released its single general-purpose 16 pin chip, the 4004, in November 1971. It had a clock speed of 740 KHz and used 2,300 transistors. The instruction cycle was 8 clock cycles, or 10.8 microseconds. It had ports for ROM, RAM, and I/O, and was originally designed for use in a calculator. Its instruction set architecture had been inspired by the DEC PDP-8. Interestingly, the little 4004 chip had at least the same processor power of the circa 1946 Eniac computer, which out-weighted it by 33 tons, The later 4040 model brought logical and compare instructions to the 4004 architecture.

The 4004 was used on the Pioneer-10 Deep Space Mission, launched in 1972. The mission studied the asteroid belt, the solar wind, Jupiter, and the outer reaches of the solar system. The computer was used to hold, decode, and distribute commands transmitted from Earth. The mission lasted until 2003, when communications was lost due to distance, a mission duration of 30 years. As of March 2011, the spacecraft was some 102 Astronomical Units (AU= 93 million miles) from the Sun, where sunlight takes 14 hours to get to. The last successful reception of telemetry was received from on April 27, 2002; subsequent signals provided no usable data. The final signal from *Pioneer 10* was received on January 23, 2003 when it was 12 billion kilometers (80 AU) from Earth.

The backup spacecraft can be seen in the Smithsonian Air & Space Museum in Washington, D. C.

Who knows what else existed in labs and research establishments at the time? Recently, a 4-bit embedded processor project that predates the Intel 4004 was declassified, a custom chip for the F-14 Tomcat fighter aircraft's Central Air Data Computer (CADC). It was not a complete single-chip design, though, and strictly speaking, did not venture into space.

The Apollo-Soyuz (joint US-Russian manned mission, circa 1975) flew with a Hewlett-Packard model HP-65 hand-held scientific calculator, used to calculate critical course-correction maneuvers. The HP calculators used a proprietary 4-bit binary coded decimal (bcd) chip, and serial-by-digit calculations.

8-bit processors

Intel 8080/8085

The 8080 was a great improvement over the prior 8008 chip, incorporating many features into the chip that required the use of external hardware with the 8008. The 8080 was an NMOS design, with 8-bit words and a 16-bit address bus. It required plus and minus 5 volts and plus and minus 12 volts. It drew 0.8 watts. The circa-1973 chip was a sequential state machine design, where the current state is a function of the previous state, and current inputs. It used around 1700 milliwatts, and, in NMOS technology, had a radiation tolerance of around 10^5 RAD.

There were four control inputs: READY, which was a wait state request, and could be held indefinitely; HOLD, which was a DMA request; INT, which was the interrupt request; and RESET, which initialized the processor by clearing the Program Counter and Interrupt Request registers, the INTR and HLDA states. The HALT is cleared, and execution begins when the RESET is removed. Control inputs were asynchronous with the processors internal clock.

The 8080 used a two-phase, non-overlapping clock. Typical cycle time was a microsecond. The phases were referred to as PHI-1 and PHI-2. State was determined by successive PHI-1 clocks. This was the minimal unit of processing activity. A machine cycle was 3, 4 ,or 5 states.

There were six timing and control outputs. The SYNC signal said that the processor status was placed on the data bus. This could then be latched externally by SYNC and-ed with clock signal PHI-1. DBIN, or data bus in, showed the bi-directional data bus was in input mode. WAIT indicated that the processor was in wait state. /WR indicated that the data bus was in write mode, and there was output on the data bus. HLDA was the hold acknowledge. The data and address busses were tri-stated at this point. INTE showed whether the CPU would respond to interrupts.

With 16 address lines, the processor could address 64k bytes of memory. The program counter and stack pointers were both 16 bits. The Program Counter held the next memory location to be fetched and executed. For the stack, a PUSH operation resulted in a decrement, and a POP operation resulted in the SP being incremented. The stack is just a first-in, first-out data structure implemented in random access memory. It is sometimes referred to as a zero-address memory, because all the action happens implicitly where the stack pointer points. There is a stack status signal that allows for a separate stack memory pace for security reasons. But, the stack resides in RAM.

There were six general purpose 8-bit registers (B, C, D, E, H, L) that could be used as three 16 bit register pairs (B-C, D-E, H-L). The accumulator was 8 bits wide, and had five associated flags. These flag bits indicated the results of the previous operation: Zero, Carry, Sign, Parity, and Auxiliary Carry. The Arithmetic Logic Unit (ALU) could do arithmetic, logical, and rotate operations on data.

The instruction cycle is the time to fetch and execute an instruction. Depending on the number of memory accesses required, the instruction cycle was 1-5 machine cycles. The instruction fetch was one cycle, and up to four memory accesses might be required for data.

There were eleven different types of machine cycles in the 8080: Instruction fetch, or the M1 cycle, Memory (non-instruction) Read, Memory Write, I/O Read, I/O Write, Stack Read and Write, Interrupt Acknowledge, Halt Acknowledge, Interrupt Acknowledge while halted, and NULL, which was used during interrupt processing. During this state, the program counter was not incremented, the memory read signal was not generated, and an instruction was fetched from the interrupting device. More about this when we discuss interrupts.

How do we get out of a HALT state? We got in by executing a HALT instruction. We need to assert the RESET signal, the HOLD (which, when released, gets us back to HALT), and then Interrupt. Notice that HALT when interrupts are disabled is fatal. One can only turn the power off and back on again. A later invention was the non-maskable interrupt.

Interrupts enhance I/O response time, by allowing external events to interrupt the processing flow of the CPU. Like when the phone rings while I'm typing this. Sometimes you don't want to allow interrupts for a period of time, because there is a critical task to be done. A CPU can mask them off. I can turn off the phone.

In the 8080, when an interrupt occurs, the interrupting device supplies the next instruction. It better be a good one. A one byte instruction is easiest, but multi-byte instructions are possible. The Restart instruction is a good choice, because it is a one-byte subroutine call (or vector).

There are eight Restart instructions, numbered 0 to 7. They automatically go to addresses starting at 0 and incrementing by 8; Restart 7 goes to 38H. In this scheme, the interrupting device can supply one of the Restart instructions, which will jump to a fixed predetermined location, and execute the code there. We only have 8 bytes, so we probably put a JUMP instruction there. This is the concept of a vectored interrupt, using a table of vectored addresses. The Interrupt Service routine, the piece of code that does what we interrupted the flow of the processor to do, can be anywhere in memory, pointed to by the JUMP instruction we put in the fixed location table. But, two cautions: The table of addresses in memory must have proper contents before an interrupt occurs, and the proper code must reside at the target address. This is part of the initialization process. The state machine doesn't care if we load something there or not – it will use the contents of memory as the instruction to be executed, and, as Von Neumann allows, we execute data (or stack contents).

One common problem was to only load the interrupt vectors that were being used. Then, invariably, a "rogue" interrupt caused by noise would vector through the non-initialized memory to a random location, and begin executing data, causing vast resources to be expended upon debugging (and many bad words to be said).

The Intel approach to Input-Output is to use a separate I/O address space and I/O instructions. This does not preclude using memory-mapped I/O. The 8080 had 256 inputs and 256 outputs, each one byte wide. (Thus, the I/O address was 8 bits). The Accumulator register held the I/O address.

Once the 8080 was accepted by the microcomputer community, other variations of the hardware appeared by Intel and their competitors. The 9080 was AMD's version of the 8080, with a correction made to an oversight in the Intel design. In the 8080, the setting of the Auxiliary Carry bit during subtraction was not correct.

The 8080 chip found use about a variety of space missions, including NASA's OSS-1, 2, and 3 Shuttle-attached pallets, Hubble Space Telescope, International Sun-Earth Explorer, Seasat, and the French Meteosat program and OTS missions. The OSS attached pallets onboard the Space Shuttle were not exposed to the harsh environment of space for extended periods. The pallets accommodated multiple experiments and instruments. Seasat operated for 105 days in orbit, when it suffered a catastrophic electrical system failure.

The 8085 was an advanced version of the 8080. It had two new instructions to enable/disable three added interrupt pins (and the serial I/O pins). It also featured simplified hardware that required only a single +5V supply, and clock-generator and bus-controller circuits on the chip. It was binary compatible with the 8080, but required less supporting hardware, allowing simpler and less expensive microcomputer systems to be built. The 8085 found use in several space missions, including NASA's OSS series. It was also used on the 1997 JPL Mars Pathfinder Rover *Sojourner*. This Rover didn't stray far from its lander. The attitude control system on the WIRE spacecraft used an 80C85, as did the FAST and XTE missions.

Z-80

The Zilog Z-80 was designed by Frederico Faggin after he left Intel, and released in1976. While at Intel, Faggin designed or led the design teams for all of Intel's early processors: the 4004, the 8008, and particularly, the revolutionary 8080.

The Z-80 was binary compatible with the 8080. Faggin intended it to be an improved version of the 8080. It could execute all of the 8080 operating codes as well as 80 new instructions (including 1-, 4-, 8-, and 16-bit operations, block I/O, block move). Because it contained two sets of data registers, it supported fast context switches.

The memory interface was vastly simplified over the 8080's, since the CPU generated its own DRAM refresh signals without requiring external circuitry. The Z-80 flew on numerous space missions, including the popular Shuttle attached payloads on the OSS pallets.

8051

The Intel 8051 was developed as an embedded processor by Intel in 1980. Embedded processors can operate with fewer external parts, and the 8051 includes memory and Input/Output on the same chip. Now, many manufacturers offer versions of the 8051, and it is widely used in college-level embedded systems courses. The most recent instantiations of the design include IP (intellectual property) core versions, for implementation within FPGA's (field programmable gate arrays) that need one or more cpu's. Why re-invent the wheel, when the 8051 comes with a development history, loyal following, and support tools? The 8051 found application on NASA's environmental satellites Aqua and Aura.

Motorola 6800

The Motorola 6800 chip was introduced in 1975. A much simpler architecture than the Intel chips, it had72 instructions, and a single 16-bit index register. There were one to three bytes per instruction. The index register modifies operand addresses during execution, typically for vector/array operations. Before index registers and without indirect addressing, array operations were complicated to implement.

The 6800 was the first in a family of microprocessors and support chips. It had 8-bit wide data, and a 16-bit wide address bus. It only required a single 5-volt power supply, and used a simple two-phase clock source. It was a synchronous design, so the clock could not be stopped or changed. It had a problem WAIT-ing for an external operation. A machine cycle was defined as a Phase1 and a Phase 2 clock. During Phase1, the address for the instruction fetch was placed on the bus. During Phase2, the instruction was read. On the next Phase1, the instruction was executed. There were two sets of accumulators, A and B. All Input/Output was memory mapped; no separate I/O instructions were provided. The status register contained bits to indicate carry/borrow, overflow, zero, negative, and half-carry, as well as an interrupt mask.

All interrupts were vectored. The 6800 included a non-maskable interrupt. This fetched the contents from memory addresses FFFC and FFFD into the program counter, effectively forcing a jump to the contents of those addresses. THE NMI was the highest priority interrupt. Interrupts were always serviced after the completion of the currently executing instruction. The normal interrupt vectored through locations FFF8 and FFF9. The 6800 had a software interrupt instruction. Executing this instruction was just like an external interrupt occurring. The difference was, it was synchronous to program execution. The program vectored through locations FFFA and FFFB. The RESET signal can be considered an interrupt. With a positive going edge on the reset line, program accessible registers were cleared, and hardware was initialized. The interrupt mask bit was then set, locking out other interrupts. Then the machine vectors through memory locations FFFE and FFFF. There was also a WAIT instruction, that caused the processor to stop processing and wait for a hardware interrupt.

Control signals were relatively simple. The VMA line indicated a valid memory address on the address bus. The R/W signal indicated whether the bus was doing a read or write operation. BA indicated the bus was available, as the processor had tri-stated its data and address bus and control lines. An Enable signal was available from AND-ing Phase1 of the clock, and the VMA signal. 6800 chips were widely used on the Shuttle-attached pallets on the OSS missions.

RCA 1802

The 1802 was released by RCA in 1976. It was quite a different architecture than other contemporary cpu's, and was produced in complementary metal oxide semiconductor (CMOS) technology, which is both low-power and radiation resistant, though susceptible t electrostatic discharge. It is also a static logic design, which could operate at a wide range of clock speeds down to zero. The architecture has also been implemented in silicon-on-sapphire technology which greatly improves its radiation hardness.

It had a register file of 16 registers of 16 bits each. Using the SEP instruction, one could select any of the registers to be the program counter or index register.

A few commonly used subroutines could be called quickly by keeping their address in one of the 16 registers. Before a subroutine returned, it jumped to the location immediately preceding its entry point so that after the RET instruction returned control to the caller, the register would be pointing to the right value for next time. An interesting variation was to have two or more subroutines in a ring so that they were called in round-robin order.

The RCA 1802 is one of the first RISC chips. RISC (Reduced Instruction Chip Computer) refers to an optimization technique where the instruction set is streamlined for performance. However, it s makes the chip more difficult to program. The 1802's radiation tolerance is around 10^5 RAD, with a power consumption of 30 milliwatts.

The 1802 was reported to be used on JPL's Voyager and Galileo space probes. Multiple units were definitely used on Galileo, but there is some question about its use on the other two spacecraft. Prior to Voyager, JPL was using simple flight computers, purpose-built, and not based on a microprocessor architecture. This Command Computer System (CCS) architecture was 18-bit.

The Voyager spacecraft, previously called Mars-Jupiter-Saturn-77, were launched during a unique opportunity in 1977 to take them past the maximum number of outer planets. They went on to explore Jupiter, Saturn, Neptune, and Uranus before heading off to interstellar space. The Voyager's are now some 13 light-hours beyond the Sun, and still returning data. In 2010, the returned data from Voyager-2 was garbled, leading to an investigation that showed the most likely cause was a flipped memory bit. Adjustments were made to the ground equipment to accommodate this, and the spacecraft continues to return useful data some 33 years after launch.

The 1802 was also quite popular with the builders of the OSCAR series of amateur spacecraft.

MCS-51

This 8-bit Intel product is a microcontroller. It was developed from the 8048 as an embedded control processor by Intel in 1980. Embedded processors can operate with fewer external parts, and the 8051 includes memory and Input/Output on the same chip. They had serial I/O plus dual timers, 4k of ROM, and 128 bytes of RAM. They operated up to 16 MHz, and came in ROM-less versions (8031), and in CMOS. The 8051 has been used on NASA's environmental satellites Aqua and Aura. The UT69RH051 is a rad-hard 8051 from Aeroflex. It is rated for a total dose of 1 million rads, and is latch-up immune. It implements the 8051 instruction set, and has three 16-bit timers, on-chip ram, 32 I/O lines, supports 7 interrupts, and has an integral serial communications channel.

Fairchild F8

The F-8 was introduced in 1975 by Fairchild Semiconductor. One of the chief designers was Robert Noyce, who went on to found Intel Corporation. Interestingly, the processor had no stack pointer, program counter, nor address bus. Addresses were maintained in the address pointer register. The chip also had 64 bytes of scratchpad memory and 64 registers. It was initially produced as a two-chip version, with a single chip implementation by Mostek in 1977. The 2-chip version did not need additional support chips.

The F-8 found application onboard NASA's Payload Assist Module (PAM-D). This was, essentially, an upper stage for the space shuttle, allowing the shuttle to launch a payload into a geosynchronous or higher orbit. The PAM-D was a Delta-class solid-fuel module, providing the same performance to higher orbit as a Delta rocket launched from the ground. Since the operation of the PAM on orbit was only a matter of minutes, the usual issues of radiation resistance were not all that applicable. The associated support electronics and equipment for the launch was carried in the Shuttle bay, returned, and reused. It was also used on the Tiros weather satellites, and the similar military weather satellites, the Block5D.

Contemporary 8-bit processors

There are still jobs an 8-bit processor can do well. Existing code that is proven correct can be re-used on newer but functionally equivalent hardware. Thus, 8-bit processors have survived, and new ones continue to appear. The Intel 8051 and Zilog Z-80 still exist in many variations, and as an IP (Intellectual Property) core for FPGA's. Freescale Semiconductor has their Motorola 8-bit clones, the 68HC08 and -11. PIC has a full line of embedded 8-bit processors. Other company's such as Atmel and NEC have similar products as well.

A PIC-18 microcontroller was used on NASA's SuitSat-1 in February 2006. SuitSat -1 was an actual Russian spacesuit, beyond its useful life, instrumented, inflated, and cast off from the

International Space Station. The controller board used a Microchip PIC18F8722 8-bit microcontroller, MCP9800 temperature sensor, and MCP6022 op-amps.

An example of a contemporary 8-bit soft core, instantiated in an FPGA, is the SpaceRISC8 Microcontroller, which has the instruction set of the PIC16F86 chip, from Microchip Technology, Inc.

12-bit Processor

Intersil 6100A

The 6100A from Harris Corp. was a circa 1975 12-bit microprocessor originally released by Intersil. The chip used the DEC PDP-8 instruction set with 90 single word instructions. It had a program counter register, a 12-bit accumulator, AC, and an MQ register (for multiply and divide operations). As there was no stack, subroutine return addresses were stored in the first word of the subroutine. Conditionals allowed the next instruction to be skipped. There was one maskable interrupt. At interrupt, the CPU stored the current address at location zero in memory, and jumped indirectly through address one. The chip was a static design.

Limited to 4096 words of memory by the 12-bit architecture, the 6100 architecture was extended by the associated 6102. This added three address lines, for a total of 32k words, by paging. It also supported DMA, and added a timer. The 6101 Parallel Interface Element (PIE) chip was an I/O port. It had dual, 12-bit input and output ports. Up to 31 of the chips per system could be used. The 6103 was a parallel I/O device with DMA, that could be used to refresh DRAM. All of these chips had their own unique instructions. The 6402 was a UART. Intersil provided matching SRAM (12-bits) and PROM.

The Intersil 6100A was used on instruments on NASA's Solar Maximum Mission (SMM) spacecraft, launched in 1980. . It was low-power (about 50 milliwatts), and widely used in high-reliability applications. It was available in military-spec versions, and was dual sourced by Intersil. The radiation tolerance was 10^5 RADS.

16-bit Processors

This section presents a history and architecture of 16 bit microprocessors in space These were generally derived from the 8-bit microprocessors of the time, and had, obviously, a larger word size, but also addressed more memory, and introduced floating point computation capability. Multiply and divide instructions became common.

Floating point provides a different representation of numbers than integer, trading accuracy for dynamic range. It is an analog to engineering or scientific notation, having a fixed precision mantissa, and a power of the base (2, in this case). Necessarily, different hardware than that used for mathematical operations on integers is required.

Intel 8086 family

Some members of Intel's 16-bit 8086 processors found application in spacecraft, using in the cmos version of the chip. The HealthSat-II mission used two of the 80c186, and an 80c188. PoSat-1 used an 80c186.

The 80186 is a microcontroller version of the 8086, incorporating an integral clock generator, dma channels, interrupt controllers, and chip selects. This greatly reduced the number of chips in a design.

The 80188 is a 80186, with an 8-bit external bus. This allows for less expensive 8-bit wide memory to be used, at the cost of time. Each memory word access (16 bits) required two 8-bit wide sequential memory accesses.

TI-9900

The Texas TI-9900 processor was used on the Landsat-D spacecraft. TI introduced the chip in 1976. It was a chip version of Texas Instrument's 990 minicomputer. It had 16-bit words, but a 15-bit address bus. There were only three internal registers, but it used the concept of a workspace, where the general purpose registers were kept in memory. The WP register pointed to this workspace. This speeded up context switches, since only the value in the WP register needed to be changed. All illegal (undefined) op codes automatically executed as a NOP, which cannot be said for most processors of the time. The 9900 also had an Execute instruction. The 9900, implemented in I^2L technology had an inherent radiation tolerance of 10^7 RAD, and drew around 500 milliwatts. (the author fondly remembers the TI-9900 chip, as it was the first microprocessor system he personally purchased and built). A TI-9900 was used on the GRO mission.

DEC LSI-11

The Digital Equipment Corporation LSI-11 was a chip-version of the 16-bit minicomputer architecture of the PDP-11. DEC's first microprocessor, it was introduced in 1975 as a multi-chip set. It was a micro-coded device, and the microcode could be used to extend the instruction set. Floating point operations were supported. It was not quite the same architecture as the standard PDP-11 microcomputer.

The members of the chip set were the Data chip, the Control chip, and one or more MICROM memory chips. The Data chip implemented the instruction execution path of the LSI-11 chip set. The Data chip operated under the control of microwords fetched from the MICROM chips by the Control chip. The Control chip provided address generation for the MICROM chips and control for external data access. The MICROM chip was a high speed 512 x 22 bit ROM which supplied microinstructions to the Data and Control chips under the direction of the Control chip. Up to four

MICROMs were in a system Two of these implemented the base PDP-11 instruction set; a third was required to implement the extended (EIS) and floating (FIS) instruction sets.

The LSI-11 was used on the Shuttle attached OSS pallets, Hubble Space Telescope, and NASA's Gamma Ray Observatory (GRO) mission.

1750A

The MIL-STD-1750 lays out a formal definition of a 16-bit instruction set architecture. It does not specify an implementation. The standard allows for memory mapping up to 2^{20} 16-bit words. There are 16 general purpose registers. Some can be used as index registers, some as base registers. Any register can be used as the stack pointer. Both 16 and 32-bit integer arithmetic are supported, as well as 32- and 48-bit floating point.

There are many implementations of the 1750A architecture, including several that are built as radiation-hardened pieces.

The preferred language for the 1750A was Jovial, an Algol language variant; later, ADA and c were used as well. The 1750A is found in many aircraft and missile applications by the United States Armed Forces and their allies. A quick list of examples include the USAF F-16 and −18, the AH-64D helicopter, and the F-111. The architecture is also used by the Indian Space Research Organisation (ISRO), and the Chinese Aerospace industry. In 1996, the 1750A architecture was declared obsolete for future military projects.

The 1750A found applications in many space projects, including NASA's Earth Observation Satellites (EOS) Aqua, Terra, and Aura. It was used on ESA missions Cluster and Rosetta. JPL used seven of the processors on the Cassini Mission to Saturn, and more units on Mars Observer and Huygens veyor. It was used on the Clementine spacecraft, a NASA-Naval Research Laboratory Program to study the Moon. The 1750A was deployed on the Johns Hopkins University Applied Physics Laboratory's MSX – Midcourse Space Experiment spacecraft, which used nine. The 1750A flew on EUVE, MSTI -1, -2, & -3, Landsat-7, NEAR, and is on the GOES-13, GOES-O, and GOES–P NOAA spacecraft. The SPOT-4 mission includes a F9450, a National Semiconductor implementation. GEC-Plessy also manufactures a radiation-hard RH1750A.

Seven of the BAE-manufactured 1750A's went to Saturn on the Cassini Mission. These are part of BAE's Advanced Spaceborne Computer module (ASCM).BAE claims 200 of these modules are in orbit, in 2011.

MA3750

ESA funded the development of a space-rated 16-bit microprocessor in the early 1990's. Built by Dynex Semiconductor, the MA3750 was a multichip architecture built in CMOS/SOS technology, capable of 2 million instructions per second (mips) performance.

RTX2010

The Intersil RTX2010 was a radiation-hardened 16-bit processor organized as a stack machine. The architecture supports direct execution of the Forth language. The Forth environment can be seen as a dual-stack virtual machine. The chip has two stacks, each 256 words deep. Context switches took a single machine cycle. The interrupt latency is 4 cycles, making the processor ideal in real-time applications.

The initial implementation came in a gate array in 1983, proceeding to a direct implementation in silicon by Harris Corporation in 1988.

The RTX2010 was used in numerous spacecraft missions, including The Advanced Composition Explorer (ACE), the NEAR/Shoemaker mission, Timed, IMAGE (2000), instruments on AXAF, EOS, and EUV, MSX, XTE, Cassini, and MagSat.

Bit slice processors

Architecture

In the bit slice architecture, you can construct a processor from multiple functional modules of a smaller bit width. The practice has fallen out of favor as individual chips have become more capable, and more economical. The critical module in a bit slice design is the arithmetic logic unit (ALU) which performs the arithmetic and logical operations on data. It was usually 1 to 8 bits in width, with carry in/carry out. The next module would be a microcontroller or micro-sequencer, that would define the instruction set, and define the execution of instructions. One microcontroller and multiple arithmetic-logic units (ALU's), combined with memory allow a design of a somewhat arbitrary word width. Propagation delays in the logic provide a practical limit to word width. With 64 bit chips available in commodity, bit-slicing in hardware makes less sense. Although, in a FPGA implementation, it can provide a method of implementing non-standard word widths to accommodate peculiarities of the data structures. For example, the data from a particular instrument might well be accommodated by a 23-bit ALU.

The Galileo spacecraft's Attitude and Articulation Control System (AACS) used an Applied Technologies Advanced Computer (ATAC), a 16-bit design. The machine had 2 kilobytes of ROM and 64 kilobytes of ram. It was programmed in assembly language and HAL/s, the higher language developed for the Shuttle Program. It hosted a real-time operating system developed at Jet Propulsion Laboratory.

AMD 2900

AMD's 2900 series was a popular TTL bit-slice architecture starting in 1975. The modules were 4 bits wide. The 2901 chip was the ALU. More than 50 types of modules were available, adding functionality such as interrupts, memory control, direct memory access (dma), and error detection and correction. The designs using the 2900 series tended to have a fairly high chip count. It was Rad hard to around 107 RAD. A 16 bit machine (4 ALU modules) would dissipate about 10 watts. 2900-based flight electronics were used by the early Tracking & Data Relay system (TDRSS) satellites.

Signetics 8x300

The 8x300 was a 16-bit bit-slice microcontroller. Data could be 1 bit to 8 bits in width. It had eight 8-bit wide registers. Each instruction was executed in one cycle, which is a characteristic of a RISC architecture. Signetics 8x300 parts formed the basis for electronics on Goddard's MMS (Multi-Mission Modular Spacecraft, including SMM, Landsat, and Hubble Space Telescope, and on the Shuttle-attached OSS pallets.

Intel 3000

The Intel 3000 was a TTL (Schottky) bit slice machine, requiring about 15 watts for a 16-bit implementation. it was hard to 10^7 RAD. The chip was introduced in 1974, and each component implemented 2 bits. There were eventually 20 members of the 3000 family. The 3001 was the microcontrol unit, and the 3002 was the 20bit ALU slice. The 3214 was the interrupt controller.

DSP

This section discusses Digital Signal Processors, which specifically address audio and video class data processing.

Motorola 56000

The Motorola DSP50000 was introduced in 1986, and is still produced today. It is a 24-bit fixed point unit. It has a variation of the Harvard architecture, with one program and two data spaces. The 56001 has 512 words of on-chip program ram, and two 256 word data rams. It also has a 32 x 24 bit bootstrap ROM. It has a highly parallel architecture, with 62 instructions. It is implemented in low-power CMOS technology, and includes a SCI (serial communications interface) and a synchronous serial interface. Eight of the Motorola 56001 were used on the HETE-2 mission.

TMS320C40

The Texas Instruments TMS320Cx represents a second generation DSP IEEE floating point processor. The 40 model is the first in the family. The unit includes hardware divide and square root, on chip 2 kbytes of SRAM, 128 bytes of program cache, and a boot loader. It also has two 32-bit timers, and up to 12 channels of DMA. There are 6 communication ports. It can address up to 4 gigabytes of 32-bit words. The TMS320C40 flew on Mightysat-II (4 units).

32-bit processors

The Intel 80386 architecture, with the associated 80387 floating point coprocessor, is a 32-bit extension of the 80286 series. Sandia National Laboratories developed a radiation-hard version of the Pentium. Only Intel processors of the 80386 class and later offer memory management, which is essential for implementation of modern operating systems.

The Space Station Mutiplexer/Demultiplexer uses a 80386SX with associated 80387SX floating point coprocessor with 16MHz clock. The SX model was 32 bits internally, but with a 16-bit external interface. Eight Megabytes of ram with EDAC was used. Serial digital and parallel channels, 1553 bus, optical channels, and a 300 megabyte mass storage device were employed.

The WIRE spacecraft used a 16 MHz 80386/80387 pair. WIRE had 1 megabyte of SRAM, 64 kilobytes of eeprom, and an 88 Megabytes of bulk memory. In addition, an 82380 DMA controller, and a 8251 serial controller were used. The FUSE spacecraft used an 80386/80387-16 MHz in its command and data handling, and also in its attitude control system, as did NASA's Sampex, SMEX, TRACE, and SWAS missions. The XTE spacecraft used an 80386 in its data system.

The University of Surrey (UK) MicroSat series, including UoSat-12 used the 80386EX, an embedded version of the 80386. This circa 1994 chip had a static design, meaning the clock could be slowed or stopped without the microprocessor losing state.

The 80386EX model includes the memory management features of the baseline 80386, and adds an interrupt controller, a watchdog timer, sync/async serial I/O, Direct Memory Access (DMA) control, parallel I/O and dynamic memory refresh control. These devices are DOS-compatible in the sense that their I/O addresses, dma and interrupt assignments correspond with an IBM pc board-level architecture. The DMA controller is an enhanced superset of the 8237A DMA controller. The 80386EX processor core is static.

The 80386EX includes: two dma channels, three channels of 8254 timer/counter, dual 8259A interrupt controller functionality, a full-duplex synchronous serial I/O channel, two channels of 8250A asynchronous serial I/O, a watchdog timer, 24 lines of parallel I/O, and support for dram refresh.

The circa 1989 Intel 80486 is a follow-on to the 80386/387 chips, and most significantly incorporated the functions of the central processing unit (cpu) and floating point processors on one chip.

The 80486 was used on the Hubble Space Telescope. When the orbiting telescope's Control Unit/Science Data Formatter failed on the "A" side in 2008, NASA cautiously switched to the "B" side, which contained an 80486 processor in the Science Instrument Command & Data Handling Unit. The redundant components had not been powered on since 1990. The successful initiation of the "B" side of the redundant unit restored full data functionality to the spacecraft.

The Hubble Space Telescope's DF-224 on-board computer was augmented in 1993 with a 16 MHz 80386/80387 during the First Servicing Mission in 1993. Servicing Mission 3A replaced the DF-224 with a new computer based on the 80486. The DF-224 was a 1970's design.

The Department of Energy-Sandia Labs manufactured a radiation-hard version of the Pentium chip, under a no-cost license from Intel. Partners in the program included NASA, the Air Force Research Laboratory, and the National Reconnaissance Office.

The Motorola 68000

The Motorola 68000 series of microprocessors, the basis of the original Apple computers, were 16/32 bit processors, introduced in 1979. The 68020 featured full 32-bit operation, and had a 3-stage pipeline internally. It could be coupled with an external memory management chip, the 68851. The 68000 was available in CMOS versions, resulting in a factor of 10 reduction in power consumption, and some inherent radiation resistance. The 68000 was found in many embedded controller designs.

The Motorola CPU chips could access up to 8 coprocessors, but generally only one or two were used. The 68881 (and later, 68882) floating point coprocessors were popular. These implemented the IEEE-754 floating point standard, with 80-bit registers.

The FUSE spacecraft used several 68020 processors in its instrument data subsystem, along with the associated 68882 floating point coprocessor.

The SeaStar satellite used three of the Motorola 68302 chips in a rad hard version. They were configured into a single master, multiple slave system. The 68302 was an embedded version of the 68000. The 68302 was termed an Integrated Multiprotocol Processor, or communications processor. It had a RISC core, and could support various communications protocols via downloaded firmware. It could also do Digital Signal Processing.

Thor

The Thor microprocessor, from Saab Ericsson Space, is a general-purpose, single-chip 32-bit stack-oriented RISC-architecture. The microprocessor is intended for embedded computer systems with high performance requirements in real-time applications, combined with fast execution of programs written in Ada. The chip is implemented in a radiation-hard cmos process.

32-bit RISC architecture with four stage pipeline, and a stack oriented instruction set. Fault tolerance support by concurrent error detection and correction (EDAC). Integer and IEEE standard 754 floating-point processing was supported on-chip.

Saab-Ericsson has supplied the processors for numerous European space missions and for the Ariane launch vehicles.

ARM

The ARM (Acorn RISC Machine) processor was developed for embedded applications. The Instruction Set Architecture (ISA) was licensed and implemented by a variety of companies. The ARM processor has come a long way from being an obscure British microprocessor of the 1980's to being the dominant basis for the current generation of smart phones, pda's, and tablet computers. They are also used extensively in television set-top boxes, routers, and embedded applications. The ARM architecture parts still represent the highest volume of 32-bit processors being shipped, as of this writing.

In 2010, over 6 billion ARM chips were sold, mostly into the smartphone market. ARM is the target architecture for the GNU/linux-based Android operating system, and the ARM has ports of OpenSolaris, FreeBSD, OpenBSD, NetBSD, and various GNU/linux variations, including Gentoo, Debian, Slackware, and Ubuntu, among others.

ARM is an Instruction Set Architecture (ISA) specification. It is instantiated in silicon by numerous companies under license. ARM Holdings PLC, a British Multinational company, is the inheritor of the intellectual property (IP) of the 32-bit CPU design, and licenses its use worldwide. The products include the licensable intellectual property for the ARM7, ARM9, ARM11, and the Cortex series. Derivative products include the StrongARM, the Freescale series, the Xscale, the Snapdragon, Samsung's Hummingbird, the A4 and A5 by Apple, and Texas Instruments products incorporating digital signal processing functionality, among others. This is similar to the situation with Intel's ISA-32, with chips of that architecture built by Intel, and chips with a different implementation of the architecture built by AMD and others. The Intel ISA-16 and ISA-32 addressed the desktop and server market, but embedded versions were also available.

The architecture is load/store with no memory reference instructions. The load/store operand is a register (32-bit) or an immediate constant. These operations may specify operand increment or decrement, pre- or post- operation. There is a load/store- multiple feature, essentially a block data transfer, but it affects interrupt response, because it is not interruptible. A three-operand format is used. The hardware includes a barrel shifter that one operand always goes through. A barrel shifter is a combinatorial circuit that takes no clock cycles for its operation. The instruction execution process used a 3-stage pipeline. A Booth algorithm hardware multiplier was used.

The ARM Cortex processors are the latest in the 32-bit series, and extend into multicore and 64-bit models for higher performance. There are three basic models of the Cortex processors, targeting different applications areas. These are provided as licensable products by ARM, Ltd., and produced by multiple chip manufacturers.

Cortex M addresses microcontrollers. There are currently four models, the Cortex-M0, 1, 2, and 3. All are binary compatible. The M0 is based on the ARMv6 The Thumb and Thumb-2 instruction subsets are supported. Cortex-M does not support the instruction and data caches, or the coprocessor interface, and has only a 3-stage pipeline. Silicon Space Technology produces a rad hard ARM Cortex M0. Single event upsets are mitigated by on-chip EDAC.

The Surrey Satellite Technology Nanosat Applications Platform (SNAP-1) was launched on June 28, 2000. The onboard computer (OBC) is based on Intel's StrongArm SA-1100 with 4 Mbytes of

32-bit wide EDAC protected SRAM. The error correction logic corrects 2 bits in every 8 using a modified Hamming code and the errors are "washed" from memory by software to prevent accumulation from multiple single-event upsets. There is 2 Mbytes of Flash memory containing a simple bootloader. The bootloader loads the application software into SRAM.

The Surrey Satellite Technology Nanosat Applications Platform (SNAP-1) was launched on June 28, 2000. The onboard computer (OBC) is based on Intel's StrongArm SA-1100 with 4 Mbytes of 32-bit wide EDAC protected SRAM. The error correction logic can correct 2 bits in every 8 using a modified Hamming code and the errors are "washed" from memory by software to prevent accumulation from multiple single-event upsets. There is 2 Mbytes of Flash memory containing a simple bootloader which loads the application software into SRAM.

The NanoMind A712D is an Arm-basedonboard computer for Cubesats. It uses as 32-bit ARM cpu, with 2 megabytes of RAM, and 8 megabytes of flash memory. It can also support a MicroSD flash card. It has a Can bus and a I²C interface. It comes with an extensive software library and real time operating system. Special applications, such as attitude determination and control code are available. It is tolerant to temperatures form -40 to 85 degrees C, but is not completely rad-hard.

Mars Helicopter Scout
The next Mars mission in 2021 will include the 2020 Rover, which has a robotic helicopter. It will be an eye-in-the-sky, looking out for hazards, planning a path, and see things that the rover's camera can't. It will be autonomous in operation. It is a technology demonstration, planned to fly five times, during the early mission. The copter blades are a meter in diameter, and it has two counter-rotating sets. Compasses can't work on Mars due to the low magnetic field, so it will use solar tracking abd inertial guidance. It will have its own solar panels. It is carried under the rover. It is dropped to

the ground, and the rover moves some distance away so it can ascend. It runs linux.

SPARC

The Scalable Processor Architecture (SPARC) is an open architecture, based on the Berkeley RISC. In contrast to the specification level of the MIPS processor, SPARC processors are instruction set compatible, and may be hardware compatible. In addition, the Bus specification and the reference MMU specification are usually adhered to by implementers. Multiple vendors support SPARC in different technologies. By early 1991, over 36 SPARC implementations were in existence, from at least 8 vendors.

The SPARC architecture relies on the register window architecture, which provides a hardware mechanism for procedure calling, reduces access to memory, and is configurable for fast context switching.

Exception handling depends on whether an internal or external event is occurring. An internal event is synchronous, and response is immediate, where the currently executing instruction is aborted before the processor changes state. An external event, occurring asynchronously, allows the currently executing to complete. Interrupt latency ranges from 3-7 cycles.

The SPARC memory management scheme includes an address space identifier bit field, which identifies the memory access types as user or supervisor instruction or data fetches (4 types).

The SPARC reference MMU specifies a 32 bit virtual to 36 bit physical address space translation, with support for multiple contexts, and page level protection mechanisms.

ERC-32

The ERC32 is a radiation-tolerant 32-bit RISC processor for space applications. It was developed by Temic (now Atmel) for the European Space Agency. Two versions were manufactured, the ERC32 Chip Set (Part Names: TSC691, TSC692, TSC693), and the ERC32 Single Chip (Part Name: TSC695). These implementations follow SPARC V7 specifications. Cache and MMU functions are not included. Implementations went from a 3-chip set in the 1990's to a single chip version by the end of the decade. Support for the chipset version of the ERC32 has been discontinued. The LEON processor is the follow-on, and supports the SPARC V8 specification.

The VHDL models are distributed under the open source gnu lesser general public license. The architecture is supported by the languages Ada and c.

The Atmel AT697 is a SPARC Version 8 processor, implementing ESA's LEON2 fault-tolerant architecture. It includes the integer and floating point cpu's, caches, and a memory controller. It is rated at 90 mips. It has a power consumption of under a watt, at 100 MHz. The earlier TSC695F product was based on the SPARC Version 7 architecture. These devices a rated for a total radiation dose of greater than 300 krad, and are latch-up immune to 70-90 MeV/mg/cm^3.

Interestingly, Atmel also offers space-rated DSP (digital signal processing) chips, pin-compatible with commercial products. These are 32-bit floating point products.

RISC-V

RISC-V is an open source instruction set architecture originating from U. C. Berkeley and based on the MIPS architecture, also from

42

Berkeley. The implementation can be in FPGA format, with the RISC-V Cores or SoC's downloaded from GITHUB. There is a compliance suite that the core SOC has to demonstrate before it can be label RISC-V. This is developed and maintained by the RISC-V Foundation, which currently has more than 100 members. The draft specification is also maintained on GitHub.

In addition to the basic ISA, you can add custom features to your implementation. You can make a system on a chip, with dedicated I/O, and you could do multi-core. The RISC-V foundation says, "using an open-source ISA offers greater flexibility, but it does not include any processor designs. It is up to the licensee to develop a custom processor or license one from another IP vendor, such as SiFive, which would then include some form or license and/or royalty fees to the IP vendor.

A series of open source software tools has been developed for the architecture. This is called the RISC-V Software Ecosystem, and includes the legacy tools for the MIPS processor.

These include C compilers, including GCC, debugging tools, boot loaders, kernels and operating systems, multiple simulators, debugging tools, the Forth kernel, and the GNU Eclipse IDE's. Kernels include linux, RTEMS, and others. Operating systems include Fedora, Debian, openSUSE, open Embedded, FreeBSD, NetBSD, etc.

You can fabricate your own RISC-V, or you can buy a commercial chip. There are currently 5 hardware vendors, with more coming along. The manuals for these devices are available on the RISC-V website.

The RISC-V implementation can also be made Arduino compatible. For example, the Crowd Supply HiFive1 part, running a 320 MHz clock. The chip has 16k of L1 cache, 16k of data sram, and included debugging support. There are a wide variety of I/O devices available, such as UART's, QSPI, PWM, and timers. This approach was used by Intel in it's Arduino-101 design, which was x86-based. What this approach provides is a Arduino-compatible processor, using a vast ecosystem of hardware, software, and hands-on expertise. The difference is, the "Arduino" is now a 32-bit (or 64-bit) MIPS architecture. You don't need to consider that when you implement a system. Just program it in c using the Arduino libraries. The HiFive1 product from CrowdSupply is an Arduino-compatible board, using a RISC-V architecture, The FE310 chip it uses, from SiFive, is a system-on-a-chip, very basic, and does not address external memory.

The specs on the board are impressive. The E310 cpu is 32-bit, and can run at 320 MHz. There is a 16k I-cache, a 16k data sram, and an associated debug module. On-chip peripherals include UART's, PWM's, and timers. I can be powered from a USB port. There are 19 digital I/O lines and an SPI interface. It can address up to 128 megs of external flash. There is also a 64-bit version, that requires a larger capacity logic device. Including a floating point unit or graphics processing requires even more capacity. If we want to push the edge of the envelope, we can consider multi-processor or multicore architecture on one chip.

What you get when you download a RISC-V IP you get a library of instruction set architecture. You can then program that into an FPGA. The instruction set download is free. The FPGA is not. In the end, the capability you get is less expensive than other methods.

RISC-V implementations in FPGA's

There have been multiple implementations of the RISC-V so far, and more are coming.

HiFive-1

The Arduino HiFive-1 is a RISC-V board from Arduino.org. It was announced just before the Maker Faire Bay Area - 2017. It implements the RISC-V 32-bit architecture in a SiFive E310 SoC. It runs at 320 MHz, with an embedded wifi and bluetooth capability. So, what we have is a 32-bit Arduino architecture presented to the user, while inside, all that runs on a RISC-V MIPS architecture. The Arduino user does not need to be aware of the guts – not an Arm but a MIPS architecture. In building and running code, it is an "Arduino," albeit on steroids.

You can buy this as a hardware board. At vendor Sparkfun, it is currently listed at under $68. It can support a JTAG connection via usb. It has 128 Mb of flash memory, and a boot loader in OTP memory. It can be powered from the usb connection, or a 7-12 volt external supply. It supports Arduino shields, and uses SPI, a UART connection, and standard digital 32 GPIO's at 3.3 or 5 volts. The board supports SPI, PWM, I2C, and interrupts. It comes with a SDK.

It can be programmed in C, or RISC-V assembly, using GCC toolchains. The loader/debugger is located in flash.

HiFive Unleashed

This board uses the Freedom U540 Core, a 5-core MIPS architecture. It is implemented on the U540 SoC. It has 8 Gbytes of memory with ECC, and a gigabit ethernet port. There is 32 Mbytes of flash, and it accepts a MicroSD card for non-volatile storage. It is instantiated in a 28 nm process SOC. The board supports JTAG, and has a boot rom.

There are four of the U54 cores, and a single E51 core, all 64 bits, connected by their TileLink fabric. External memory in DDR3 or DDR4 is supported. The E51 core supports hardware performance monitoring as part of the privileged architecture. The E54 cores all include floating point and virtual memory.

For I/O it supports ChipLink, QSPI, I2C, PWM, and has two UARTs. and 16 GPIO's. There are 53 global, and 7 priority interrupts.

Each U54 core has its own private L1 instruction and data caches, which are 8-way set associative, and 32k in size. The E51 core has a 2-way set-associative, 16k instruction cache.
Mode select pins allow for booting from one of several sources. The zeroth stage boot loader looks to a on-chip rom. The first stage boot loader uses the DDR memory. The Berkeley Boot Loader has emulation for soft instructions, and "the User Payload" is used to get to Linux. You can boot from a MicroSD card. The reset vector is located at 1004H. DMA is supported on the various cores.
As of this writing, the HiFive Unleased board is available for $999.

Rad-Hard MIPS architecture and their Space Missions

Once we leave the vicinity of our home planet, conditions deteriorate quickly. The major issue is radiation, since we are outside of safety of the trapped radiation belts, which provide some protection. This is the major challenge, but there are many known ways to mitigate this problem. Then, there is the thermal problem. We're going somewhere that's hotter (sun-ward), or colder. A big issue is the mission duration. It takes years to get to some of the outer planets, and even if the system is powered off, there can be events that will cause it not to wake up. Missions outside the rather friendly environment of near-Earth face additional challenges that must be addressed.
Aeroflex Leon

The LEON project was started by the European Space Agency (ESA) in late 1997 to develop a high-performance processor to be used in European space projects. The objectives for the project were to provide an open, portable, and non-proprietary processor design, capable to meet future requirements for performance, software compatibility, and low system cost. To maintain correct operation in the presence of single event upsets (SEU's), extensive error detection and error handling functions were needed. The goals were to detect and tolerate one error in any register without software intervention, and to suppress effects from Single Event Transient (SET) errors in combinational logic.

The LEON family includes the first LEON1 VHSIC Hardware Description Language design that was used in the LEONExpress test chip developed in 0.25 µm technology to prove the fault-tolerance concept. The second LEON2 VHDL design was used in the processor device AT697 from Atmel and various system-on-chip devices. These two LEON implementations were developed by ESA. Gaisler Research, now Aeroflex Gaisler, developed the third LEON3 design and the fourth generation LEON, the LEON4 processor.

A LEON processor can be instantiated in programmable logic such as an FPGA or an ASIC. LEON processors are available as soft IP cores

All processors in the LEON series are based on the SPARC-V8 RISC architecture. LEON2(-FT) has a five-stage pipeline while later versions have a seven-stage pipeline. LEON2 and LEON2-FT are distributed as a system-on-chip design that can be modified using a graphical configuration tool.

The standard LEON2 includes an interrupt controller, debug support hardware, 24-bit timers, a UART, a 16-bit I/O port, and a memory controller.

The LEON3, LEON3FT, and LEON4 cores are typically used together with the GRLIB IP Library. While the LEON2 distributions contain one design that can be used on several target technologies, GRLIB contains several template designs, both for FPGA development boards and for ASIC targets that can be modified using a graphical configuration tool similar to the one in the LEON2 distribution. The LEON/GRLIB package contains a larger number of cores compared to the LEON2 distributions and also include a plug and play extension to the on-chip AMBA bus. IP cores available in GRLIB include a 32-bit SDRAM controller, and pci bridge with dma, a 10/100/100 ethernet MAC, 8/16/32-bit wide prom and sram controller, 16/32/64 bit wide DDR/DDR@ memory controllers, a USB 2.0 host, and a CAN bus, spi, I2C, ATA controllers, a timer, interrupt controller, and general purpose I/O port.

The term LEON2/LEON2-FT refers to the LEON2 system-on-chip design, which is the LEON2 processor core together with the standard set of peripherals available in the LEON2(-FT) distribution. Later processors in the LEON series are used in a wide range of designs and are therefore not as tightly coupled with a standard set of peripherals. LEON3 and LEON4 refers to only the processor core, while LEON/GRLIB is used to refer to the complete system-on-chip design.

The LEON2-FT processor is the single event upset (seu) tolerant version of the LEON2 processor. Flip-flops are protected by triple modular redundancy (TMR) and all internal and external memories are protected by error detection and correction (edac) or parity bits. Special license restrictions apply to this IP (distributed by ESA).

The LEON3 is a synthesizable VHDL model of a 32-bit processor compliant with the SPARC V8 architecture. The model is highly configurable, and particularly suitable for system-on-a-chip (SOC) designs. The full source code is available under the GNU GPL license, allowing use for any purpose without licensing fee. LEON3 is also available under a proprietary license, allowing it to be used in proprietary applications.

There are several differences between the two LEON2 processor models and the LEON3. LEON3 includes SMP support and a seven-stage pipeline, while LEON2 does not support SMP and has a five-stage pipeline.

The LEON3FT is a fault-tolerant version of the standard LEON3 SPARC V8 Processor. It has been designed for operation in the harsh space environment, and includes functionality to detect and correct single event upset (SEU) errors in all on-chip RAM memories. The LEON3FT processor support most of the functionality in the standard LEON3 processor, and adds Register file SEU error-correction of up to 4 errors per 32-bit word, Cache memory error-correction of up to 4 errors per tag or 32-bit word, Autonomous and software transparent error handling. There is no timing impact due to error detection or correction. It is a Static design, using a 2.5 volt supply. It supports the IEEE-754 floating point standard.

The LEON3FT core is distributed together with a special FT version of the GRLIP IP library. Only netlist distribution is possible.

A FPGA implementation called LEON3FT-RTAX is proposed for critical space applications. It is tolerant to a total dose of $3x10^5$ rads, and can withstand SEU to 10^8 mev-cm2/mg.

In January 2010, the fourth version of the LEON processor was released. It has static branch prediction added to pipeline, optional level-2 cache, 64-bit or 128-bit path to AMBA AHB interface, and higher performance possible (claimed by manufacturer: 1.7 DMIPS/MHz as opposed to 1.4 DMIPS/MHz of LEON3).

The Real Time Operating systems (RTOS's) that support LEON are RTLinux, PikeOS, eCos, RTEMS, Nucleus, ThreadX, VxWorks, LynxOS, POK, a free ARINC653 implementation released under the BSD license, and embedded linux.

Star-Dundee, a U.K. Company, has developed a SPARCv8 LEON-FT architecture chips named the AT7913E. It includes memory management, a floating point unit, and a 1553 , ethernet, and CAN bus interface. It is low power, and radiation tolerant to 300 krad total dose.. It includes a debug port, and has internal memory, that can be expanded externally. It includes Spacewire interfaces, and an integral spacewire router.

MIPS

Meaning "microprocessor without interlocking stages", the MIPS architecture was the brainchild of John Hennessy at Stanford University. It was produced by multiple manufacturers, and addressed the workstation market. MIPS, the company, was eventually bought by SGI. MIPS was the keeper of the architectural specification of the chips, with various company's producing variants.

There were several architectural models of the MIPS chip. The R-2000 was a 32-bit load/store machine with associated MMU and floating point chips. The R-3000 is also 32-bit, but was produced in various versions for the embedded market. The R-4000 was a 64-bit machine with integral coprocessors.

The MIPS R3000 is a 32 bit architecture with separate R3010 floating point unit. Thirty two 32 bit registers are included on-chip. The pipeline is 5 stages in length. Branch latency is 1 clock time, and load/store latency is also 1 clock. The device averages 1.25 instructions per clock. Several addressing modes are supported, including base register and 16 bit signed immediate offset. The Harvard architecture chip supports caching of 4-256k instruction or data, and instruction streaming. On the main memory side of the cache, multiprocessor support is provided by provisions to ensure cache coherency.

Separate data and instruction caches are provided. A six element deep write buffer allows for up to 6 single cycle writes in a row. The MMU divides the memory space into a 2 gigabyte user space, and a 2 gigabyte kernal/systems space. The MMU uses a 64 entry fully associative translation look-aside buffer. Externally implemented write buffers provide decoupling of write latency from cpu operations. Both big- and little-endian data formats are supported, with the mode set during reset.

Direct mapped external cache is used, with a line size of 4 words for instruction, and 1 or 4 words for data. Physical tags are kept, so that a context switch does not require a cache flush. The data and instruction caches share the same implementation. A write-thru policy is used for the data cache. A cache parity error is treated as a cache miss. Since dma as well as multiprocessing can invalidate cache contents in a system, coherent dma is used.

For cache flushing and diagnostics, there is a provision to swap the I- and D- caches. This is controlled by a bit in the status register. A load or a store cannot be executing at the time of the swap. In addition, execution must be proceeding from a non-cacheable region of memory.

The Load/Store instructions are the only ones that reference memory, and only a single addressing mode of base register plus offset is supported. Load instructions have an inherent latency of one cycle before data is available to subsequent instructions. This can cause a load delay in the pipeline. However, the pipeline always executes the instruction following the load. It is up to the compiler to ensure that the instruction following the load does not depend on the data to be loaded. If the compiler cannot rearrange the code properly, a nop is inserted as a last resort. Delayed branches are handled in the same fashion. The base instruction set is shown in the following table.

As with the R2000 architecture, 4 coprocessors are supported. These are closely coupled, synchronous units, sharing that data bus and bus transactions with the main processor. By convention, coprocessor 0 is the System control coprocessor, and coprocessor 1 is the floating point unit. In the R3000, coprocessor 0 is implemented on the same chip as the main cpu. For a coprocessor load or store operation involving memory, the main cpu handles the addressing and control, and ignores the data. Data transfers between units use the data bus. The coprocessor can initiate a stall of the main processor, if a data dependency needs to be resolved.

The MIPS processors were designed with multiprocessing in mind, using such features as physical cache, and a mode for externally generated stall and invalidate cache status inputs. Multiprocessing depends on interprocessor communication, synchronization between processes, and data coherence. A mix of hardware and software is used to address these issues.

In a simplistic multiprocessor system, duplicate tags for the D-cache can be provided. Note that I-cache issues are much simpler, since the I-cache is only filled from the memory. Except for self-modifying code, which is frowned upon. With write-through D-cache, the main memory is always consistent with the cache, and the two caches either match or they don't. During a write operation, if the second unit is snooping on the bus and sees a write to a location it has cached, it invalidates that location in its own cache. However, write-thru caches generate a lot of redundant bus traffic, because not all writes to cache need be written to main memory. With a write buffer, the situation gets more complicated, because the write buffer may need to be flushed to main memory to maintain coherency among caches.

A more sophisticated scheme uses a secondary cache with a write-back policy. Not only does the secondary cache function as a write buffer to main memory, but does the tag comparison and coherency transactions. Again, note that this level of complexity is required only for the D-cache, not the I-cache.

With physically addressed primary and secondary caches, the primary cache, on chip, is a subset of the primary cache, which is, of course, a subset of the main memory.

Families of chips have evolved to complement the CPU's, and allow the construction of full systems. One family is LSI Logic's MipSET. This family includes an interrupt controller, a DRAM controller, a data buffer, a bus controller, and DMA/Block Transfer controller. These functions will generally be integrated into the next generation chip level product. At the lower level, however, these chips reduce the overall system chip count, by eliminating the need to implement the required functionality in discrete logic. The area of support chips is one in which individual vendors of the prescribed MIPS architecture can customize and show individuality and differentiation. Another such area is derived architectures for specific application, such as embedded control, as discussed next.

Several versions of the R3000 evolved for embedded systems application. Among these are IDT's R3001 "RISController", which has a synchronous memory interface, and an on-chip DMA interface. Several variations of the 30xx with differing features have evolved.

The R3051 and R3052 controllers from IDT are essentially the same device, with the 51 variant having 4 Kbytes of I-cache, and the 52 having 8 Kbytes. Each has 2k bytes of D-cache. The R3000 core processor is incorporated. Separate versions include the functions of CR0, including MMU and TLB. The devices are packaged in small footprint, plastic packaging for low cost systems use.

MIPS in Space

An IDT R-3051 embedded controller was used on NASA's Clementine Mission. Also called the "Deep Space Program Science Experiment." Launched on January 25, 1994, the objective of the mission was to test sensors and spacecraft components under extended exposure to the space environment and to make scientific observations of the Moon and the near-Earth asteroid 1620 Geographos. The Geographos observations were not made due to a malfunction in the spacecraft.

The RHC-3000 was based on a LSI Logic implementation of the MIPS-3000 cpu, implemented in rad-hard technology by Harris Corporation. It was hard to 1 megaRad, and had a low single event upset error rate. It ran a 20 MHz clock. It could use a floating point coprocessor. As a microcontroller, it had dual dma channels, dual counter/timers, a 50 Mbps serial I/O bus, and implemented error detection and correction on the main memory and cache.

Mongoose

The Mongoose-V is a 32-bit microprocessor for space applications It is a radiation-hardened 10–15 MHz version of the MIPS 3000 architecture. The Mongoose was developed by Synova, Inc., with support from the NASA's Goddard Space Flight Center, Code 735. It is rated at 7.5 MIPS, and includes floating point support. It is fabricated in Silicon-on-Insulator technology.

The Mongoose V processor is a space-rated derivative of the LR-3000 processor of MIPS heritage. It includes a 4-kbyte instruction cache and a 2-kbyte data cache, as well as floating-point capability. However, the omission of the memory management unit forces the use of a flat memory model and precludes one of the more powerful features of advanced operating systems.

Features of the Mongoose include the MIPS R3000 Instruction Set, the R3010 Floating-point Unit, On-Chip 2KB Data Cache and 4KB Instruction Cache, and speed grades of 10MHz and 15MHz. On-chip Peripherals include Error Detection & Correction, dual Memory Protection, Timers, a Dual UART, Expansion Interrupts, a waitstate Generator, and a DRAM Controller.

Radiation Hardness is specified to be LET > 80 MeV- cm2 / mg, and the unit is Latch-up immune. It is built with a silicon-on-insulator technology.

The Mongoose-V processor first flew on NASA's EO-1 spacecraft launched in November, 2000, where it functioned as the main flight computer. A second Mongoose-V controlled the satellite's solid-state data recorder.

Other spacecraft that use the Mongoose-V include:

- NASAs Microwave Anisotropy Probe (MAP), launched in June 2001, carried a Mongoose-V flight computer similar to that on EO-1. The spacecraft measures differences in the temperature of the Big Bang's remnant radiant heat, called the Cosmic Microwave background radiation across the full sky

- NASA's X-ray Timing Explorer (XTE) mission, as the instrument telemetry controller.

- NASAs Microwave Anisotropy Probe (MAP), launched in June 2001, carried a Mongoose-V flight computer similar to that on EO-1. The spacecraft measures differences in the temperature of the Big Bang's remnant radiant heat, called the Cosmic Microwave background radiation across the full sky
- NASA's Space Technology 5 series of microsatellites

- NASA's IceSat Mission, launched into polar orbit in January 2003

- TIMED, or Thermosphere Ionosphere Mesosphere Energetic and Dynamics mission, was launched to study the dynamic of the Mesosphere and Lower Thermosphere portions of the Earth's atmosphere. The Mongoose served as the Control and Data Handling (C&DH) computer. It was launched in December 2001.

- EO-1, the Earth Observing Mission, used a Mongoose. It was launched in 2000, and is currently in extended mission mode.

- New Horizons Pluto Probe uses four Mongoose processors in its Command & Data Handling subsystem. The spacecraft was launched in 2006, and is en route to Pluto It went past Jupiter in 2007, and Saturn in 2008. it is scheduled to arrive at Pluto in 2015, and then continue into the Kipper Belt. Probably due to excessive radiation in the vicinity of Jupiter's magnetotail. On March 19, 2007 the Command and Data Handling computer experienced an uncorrectable memory error and rebooted itself, causing the spacecraft to go into safe mode.. The craft fully recovered within two days.

Harris RH3000

The RH3000 family from Harris features the MIPS architecture, and is radiation hard to a level greater than 1 MegaRad. The two-chip set includes the CPU, floating point unit, timers, bus interfaces, DMA controller, power management, and serial channels. The core logic is used under license from LSI Logic.

At the box level, Harris can put up to 21 processors with 2 gigabytes of RAM in a product called CrossStar. The chipset is also placed on a single 6U VME board called the Standard Spacecraft Processor Module. The Advanced Spacecraft Processor Module includes two processor sets and memory.

The product supports the VxWorks operating system and Tornado, and can be programmed in the c language or Ada.

RH32

The RH-32 was a radiation-hard 32-bit processor chipset developed by the USAF Rome Laboratories for the Ballistic Missile Defense Agency, and produced by Honeywell (later, TRW) for Aerospace applications. It achieves a throughput of 20 MIPS. It was a three-chip set, consisting of Central Processing Unit, Floating Point Unit, and Cache Memory

The Honeywell and TRW RH32 were developed from a MIPS R3000 model, under sponsorship of the USAF Phillips Lab at Kirkland Air Force Base in New Mexico. It features 16 kilobytes of data cache and 16 kilobytes of instruction cache. It includes four serial I/O channels, four timers, a built-in 1553 bus, 40 programmable I/O lines, and DMA capability. At a module level, the Sun M-bus is supported. The module is available in 100 K rad to one mega-rad hardness with no single-event latch-up. It incorporates IEEE-754 floating-point capability, and memory management features. The RH32 processor is an integral part of the Advanced Spaceborne Computer Module (ASCM). The RH32 supports a VxWorks operating system and the gnu-c compiler.

PowerPC

The PowerPC architecture resulted from a collaboration between Motorola and IBM. Motorola contributed the 88000 RISC architecture, and IBM threw in parts of the ROMPS, RiscPC, and Power architecture. The result was a challenge to the Intel IA-32 and IA-64.

The IBM POWER (performance optimization with enhanced RISC) architecture was circa 1990, and was designed to run the Unix variant AIX. The two processors that resulted were the RIOS I and RIOS II, before the design was blended into the PowerPC. Motorola's 88k was a risc architecture as a follow-on to their 68k cisc processor. This incorporated a 88100 cpu chip and an associated 88200 cache control chip. The cpu hosted 5 execution units and 4 pipelines. It was a Harvard architecture. There were 51 instructions, later expanded to 66, and 32 32-bit registers.

The Power-PC was 3-way superscalar, with separate integer, floating point, and branch processing. It supported out-of-order execution and hardware branch prediction. The memory management unit converted 52-bit virtual addresses to 32-bit physical addresses. The internal cache was a unified structure in the early units, moving to a separate or Harvard cache structure later. Multiple processors were supported. The PowerPC could dynamically order the load/store traffic at run time.

From a programmer's point of view, the PowerPC was a load/store architecture. All addressing was register indirect. There was an interruptible string move instruction. There were 32 general purpose integer registers, and 32 floating point registers. Byte ordering was selectable, with big-endian being the default. There were 184 instructions, and both a user and supervisor mode.

The PowerPC 601 was the first generation part, running from 50-120 Mhz. It had a unified cache of 32 kbytes. The part was used by both Apple computer and IBM. The PowerPC 602 project was to be able to execute both PPC and Intel IA-21 instruction sets, but was never completed. The PPC-603 reached 66-300 Mhz clock speeds, and introduced the Harvard cache architecture. The PPC 604 ran from 100 to 350 Mhz, and the cache size was 64k.

The PowerPC G3, models 740 and 750, featured dual caches of 32k each. The G4 introduced the AltiVec instructions. These were for multimedia data, similar to Intel's MMX extension. The AltiVec instructions, 160 in number, had their own separate 32 registers, each 128 bits wide. The G4 ran at 350 to 1100 Mhz, and went to a 7-stage pipeline.

IBM variants of the architecture included the Power3 which was a 64-bit machine and became the basis for the RS6000 servers, and the Power5, which stretched the operating frequency to 1Ghz. Motorola produced embedded versions of the PPC architecture for the automotive and communications industries. A typical MPC 5xx series embedded part included support of the PPC instruction set, integrated ram, flash, a timer, serial I/O and A/D functions.

The Power processor was proprietary to IBM . Separate integer and floating point units operate simultaneously on-chip. Separate instruction and data caches are provided, as well as a branch processor, which can provide zero-cycle branches. 184 instructions are included in the repertoire. The processor is capable of executing 4 instructions per clock. These have to be: one integer, one floating point, one branch, and one condition register operation.

The virtual address space is 2^{52} bytes in extent, mapped to a 2^{32} bit real address space. The memory bus width is 64 bits in the low end units, going to 128 bits in the higher end units.

The PowerPC features superscalar architecture, which allows simultaneous dispatching of three instructions into the three independent execution units. These execution units are the integer, the floating point, and the branch processing unit. Simultaneous instructions can execute in parallel, and complete out of order, while the hardware ensures program correctness. The on-chip branch processing unit does hardware branch prediction, with reversal. Thirty two 32 bit registers are provided, and two modes of operation (supervisor and user) are implemented.

Exceptions are particularly tricky on a machine with out of order instruction dispatch. On the PowerPC, exceptions may be recognized out-of-order, but will be handled in order. Exceptions can be precise or imprecise and synchronous or asynchronous.

The processor can dynamically order load/store memory traffic at run time, to optimize performance. Except for dependencies, reads precede stores. The PowerPC is compatible with the previous IBM POWER architecture. Extensions to the reference PowerPC definition to address specific POWER features from previous architectures are included.

Non-radiation hardened 603e's were used on NASA's Callipso (Cloud Aerosol Lidar and Infrared Pathfinder Satellite Observations) spacecraft. Four of the COTS units were used. for non-mission critical circuitry, many of the mitigation techniques can be employed, costing significantly less than a completely radiation-hard part.

PowerPC in Space

There are several variations of the PowerPC using in space flight missions.These are discussed in the following sections.

RHPPC

The U. S. Air Force funded the PowerPC 603e processor's use in space. This was a development effort at the Southwest Research Institute, and the SC603e was produced by Honeywell and Thompson. It was a 100-mips class chip, hard to a total dose of 60 kilorad. The PowerPC 603 series was also used in the General Dynamics Integrated Spacecraft Computer (ISC).

The RHPPC is a radiation hardened cpu based on the PowerPC 603 technology licensed from and manufactured by Honeywell Space Systems. It was a project of the United States Air Force Research Laboratory at Kirtland Air Force Base. The RHPPC is equivalent to the commercial PowerPC 603e processor with the minor exceptions of the phase-locked loop (PLL) and the processor version register (PVR). The RHPPC processor is compatible with the commercial PowerPC architecture, the programmers interface, and is supported by common PowerPC software tools and embedded operating systems, such as VxWorks.

The RHPPC processor generates 190 mips with its core clock at 100 MHz. The RHPPC processor completes 1.9 instructions per cycle. The RHPPC runs with a 25, 33.3, 40, or 50 MHz clock (SYSCLK) which is generated based on the PCI clock. The 60x bus clock is de-skewed on-chip by a PLL and can also be multiplied.

The RHPPC processor is a superscalar machine with five execution units: system register unit, integer unit, load/store unit, floating point unit, and branch processing unit. The dispatch unit can issue two instructions per cycle. The floating point unit has a three level deep pipeline. Out-of-order execution is supported through the use of shadow registers. The completion unit can complete two instructions per cycle in order by copying results from the shadow registers to the real registers. Independently, the branch processing unit can complete a branch each cycle. Thus, in theory, the RHPPC processor can complete three instructions per cycle. Within the RHPPC processor is a 16 kilobyte instruction and a 16 kB data cache that are 4-way set associative, and support the write-through or copy-back protocol. A cache line is fixed at eight words.

The RHPPC processor is fabricated with Honeywell's SOI-V 0.35 µm, four level metal process. It is packaged in a hermetic, 21 x 21 mm grid array package with 255 (16 x 16) leads. The leads are on 1.27 mm centers.

RAD-6000

The RAD-6000 is a 32-bit version of the IBM PowerRISC, that was the processor in the Deep Blue computer that triumphed over human chess champion Garry Kasparov. IBM's RS/6000 series of circa-1990's Unix servers used the proprietary POWER architecture, later switching to the PowerPC. POWER stood for Performance Optimization With Enhanced RISC. This represented an Instruction Set Architecture, which came out of a superscalar design of the late 1970's.

The RAD6000 radiation-hard single board computer based on the IBM risc chip, was manufactured by IBM Federal Systems. Later sold to Loral and by way of acquisition, it ended up with Lockheed Martin and currently as a part of BAE Systems.

The radiation-hardening of the original RSC 1.1 million-transistor chip to make the RAD6000's CPU was done by IBM Federal Systems Division working with the Air Force Research

Laboratory. The memory bus is 72 bits wide, to accommodate 64 data bits plus 8 bits of error correcting code. The chip includes a floating point unit. It is latchup immune, and rated at a total dose exceeding 1 megarad. The architecture was implemented in a standard cpu,. Or a ASIC or FPGA version. Computer boards were available in double or triple-redundant configurations. Each processor drew less than 12 watts of power at 20 MHz. I/O interfaces included 1553 bus, a serial (RS-422 or -232) UART, and discretes in and out.

As of June 2008 there were some 200 RAD6000 processors in space on a variety of NASA, DoD, and commercial spacecraft, including:

The *Spirit* and *Opportunity* Mars Rovers, the Mars Pathfinder Lander, the Deep Space-1 probe, Mars Polar Lander and Mars Climate Orbiter, Mars Odyssey Orbiter, the Spitzer Infrared Telescope, the Messenger probe to Mercury, the Stereo spacecraft, MIDEX (Explorer 78), Genesis and Stardust sample return missions, the Phoenix Mars Polar lander, the Dawn asteroid belt mission, the Solar Dynamics Observatory spacecraft, launched Feb 11, 2010 flying both RAD6000 and RAD-750, Coriolis, Gravity Probe B, HESSI, SMEX-lite, SWIFT, Triana, and SIRTF.

The computer has a maximum clock rate of 33 Mhz and a processing speed of about 35 mips. In addition to the CPU itself, the RAD6000 has 128 megabytes of error-correcting RAM VxWorks is supported on the RAD6000. The flight boards have selectable clock rates of 2.5, 5, 10, or 20 MHz.

The RAD750 is a radiation hardened single board computer based on a licensed version of the IBM PowerPC 750. The successor to the RAD6000, the RAD750 is manufactured by BAE Systems. It is intended for use in high radiation environments in space. The RAD750 was released for purchase in 2001 and the first units were launched into space in 2005. Software developed for the RAD6000 is upwardly compatible with the RAD750.

The cpu has 10.4 million transistors compared with the RAD6000's 1.1 million. It is manufactured using either 250 or 150 nm photolithography and has a die area of 130 mm² It has a core clock of 110 to 200 MHz and can process at 266 MIPS or more. The CPU can include an extended Level 2 cache to improve performance. Its packaging and logic functions are completely compatible with the standard PowerPC 750.

The CPU itself can withstand 2,000 to 10,000 gray (1 gray = 100 rad) and temperature ranges between –55 and 125C. It requires 5 watts. The standard RAD750 single-board system (CompactPCI board form factor) can withstand 1,000 gray and temperature ranges between –55 °C and 70 °C and requires 10 watts of power.

Maxwell's SCS-750 space computer incorporates three PPC750 chips in a voting configuration.

There are many spacecraft in operation using RAD750 computers, including:

- The Deep Impact mission to a comet, launched in January 2005, was the first to use the RAD750 computer.

- The MARS Reconnaissance Orbiter (MRO) spacecraft has a 133 MHz RAD750 in the Command and Data Handling subsystem..

- The XSS-11 small experimental satellite.

- The Fermi Gamma-ray Space Telescope, formally GLAST, launched June 11, 2008

- Two RAD750 computers are in the World View-1 satellite which provide high-resolution imaging of Earth. It is a part of the National Geospatial Intelligence Agency's NextView program. It was launched in 2007.

- The Keppler Space Telescope, launched in March 2009.

- The Lunar Reconnaissance Orbiter (LRO) launched in June 2009.

- The Wide Field Survey Explorer (WISE) launched in 2009.

- The Titan-Saturn System Mission (TSSM) spacecraft will have a 132 MHz RAD750 on board, with a scheduled launch in 2020.

- The Solar Dynamics Observatory spacecraft, launched Feb 11, 2010, includes both RAD6000 and RAD-750 processors.

By 2010, it was estimated that there were over 200 RAD750s used in a variety of spacecraft.

Freescale QorIQ

Freescale Semiconductor manufacturers a series of PowerPC-based embedded microcontrollers. These have evolved to include multicore models. In particular, the 8-core P4080 was chosen by the Fraunhofer Institute for Computer Architecture and Software Technology for their Project Muse. Muse stands for Multicore architecture for sensor-based position tracking in Space. The chosen chip can operate with up to a 1.5 GHz clock, to achieve a processing power of 60 GIPS. The chip is built on silicon-on-insulator technology for radiation tolerance. Multiple cores are used for redundancy and fault tolerance. The TMR voting circuitry is implemented in a radiation tolerant FPGA. The microcontroller contrains, besides the 8 computer cores, six gigabit ethernet channels, dual PCI express interfaces, dual Rapid I/O, and dual SpaceWire.

The Transputer

The Inmos Transputer architecture was introduced in 1985 as a single chip microcomputer architecture, optimized for parallel use in Multiple Instruction, Multiple Data (MIMD) configurations. It provided excellent and balanced inter-processor communications as well as computational ability. Transputers provided the capability to implement scalable systems. It was truly a system-on-a-chip, with processor, memory, and I/O. Timers were included internally, and the chip requires merely a crystal to derive its own clock. The timers enabled real time programming and process scheduling. Because the input clock was 5 MHz regardless of the internal rate of the Transputer, a master clock could be distributed across a board. It did not have a memory management unit. The T-800 model supported IEEE floating point.

Transputers had, in a sense, an embedded operatiing system. Tey implemented Communicating Sequential Processes by means of the Occam language. Occam supposted concurrency and interprocess communication,

The Transputer was too far ahead of its time. Update the clock speeds, and the architecture would be impressive today. It was a Microcomputer, having a cpu, memory, and I/O on one chip. External logic required was minimal. Large arrays of Transputers were easily implemented. However, like many advanced technological artifacts, it was hard to understand. It found application in many spacecraft instruments of the day, due to its monolithic design and embedded focus. The Transputer family part were available in compliance with MIL-STD-883A, and program was in progress to produce radiation-hardened versions of the 32-bit Transputer architecture. Unfortunately, less capable but easier to use processors superseded the Transputer's use.

The HETE-2 spacecraft, a follow-on to replace the lost HETE-1 spacecraft, was launched on Oct. 9, 2000. The spacecraft computer system consists of four identical processor boards: each board contains one T805 Transputer, two Motorola 56001 digital signal processors (DSP's), and 20 Megabytes of RAM. The processors are assigned to the spacecraft and science needs. The Transputer links allow for quick and efficient communications between processors. The Digital signal processors (DSP's) serve as the interface to the instruments.

The embedded instrument controller for the Coronal Diagnostic Spectrometer was prototyped at GSFC using a T222 Transputer. This instrument was a part of the SOHO/ISTP (Solar Heliospheric Observatory / International Solar-Terrestrial Physics) Program, jointly funded by the European Space Agency. This work was done as part of the Laboratory for Astronomy and Solar Physics. The flight unit, using a T800 processor, was delivered for a Summer 1995 launch. The Transputer serves as an embedded controller, orchestrating the operation of the 1024 x 1024 element CCD (charge-coupled device) sensing element. The data system on the SOHO spacecraft also uses Transputers.

The Myriade satellite platform by Astrium systems is based on the T-805 Transputer, and was in production through 2015.

CubeSats

A Cubesat is a small, affordable satellite that can be developed and launched by college, high schools, and even individuals. The specifications were developed by Academia in 1999. The basic structure is a 10 centimeter cube, (volume of 1 liter) weighing less that 1.33 kilograms. This allows a series of these standardized packages to be launched as secondary payloads on other missions. A Cubesat dispenser has been developed, the Poly-PicoSat Orbital Deployer, that holds multiple Cubesats and dispenses them on orbit. They can also be launched from the Space Station, via a custom airlock. ESA, the United States, and Russia provide launch services. The Cubesat origin lies with Prof. Twiggs of Stanford University and was proposed as a vehicle to support hands-on university-level space education and opportunities for low-cost space access.

Cubesats can be custom made, but there has been a major industry evolved to supply components, including space computers. It allows for an off-the-shelf implementation, in addition to the custom build. There is quite a bit of synergy between the Amsat folks and Cubesats. NASA supports the Cubesat program, holding design contests providing a free launch to worthy projects. Cubesats are being developed around the world, and several hundred have been launched.

Build costs can be lower than $10,000, with launch costs ranging around $100,000, a most cost-effective price for achieving orbit. The low orbits of the Cubesats insure eventual reentry into the atmosphere, so they do not contribute to the orbital debris problem.

Central to the Cubesat concept is the standardization of the interface between the launch vehicle and the spacecraft, which allows developers to pool together for launch and so reduce costs and increase opportunities. As a university-led initiative, Cubesat developers have advocated many cost-saving mechanisms, namely:

- A reduction in project management and quality assurance roles
- Use of student labor with expert oversight to design, build and test key subsystems
- Reliance on non-space-rated Commercial-Off-The-Shelf (COTS) components
- Limited or no built-in redundancy (often compensated for by the parallel development of Cubesats)
- Access to launch opportunities through standardized launch interfaces
- Use of amateur communication frequency bands and support from amateur ground stations
- Simplicity in design, architecture and objective

The approach has since been adopted by numerous universities and organizations, and to date has been used as the basis of 40 missions (as at the end of October 2008) which have been launched since 2003, with many active projects in development. High schools and individuals are also pursuing Cubesat projects. The launch cost is a major issue, but multiple Cubesats can be carried as secondary payloads on military and commercial flights.

Since the initial proposal of the concept, further efforts have been made to define internal and external interfaces made by various developers of Cubesat subsystems, products and services that have defined the Cubesat 'standard' as it is today. A core strength of the Cubesat is its recognition of the need for flexibility in the definition of standards, and since conception the standard has evolved to ensure that these design rules are as open as possible. The most significant of these further advances in definition have been for the POD systems (in order to meet launch requirements) and the modularization of the internal electronics.

The in-orbit success rate of university-led Cubesat projects (not withstanding launch failures) is around 50%; this is an understandable result of using the Cubesat as an education tool, where development itself is a learning process and in-orbit failure is a disappointment but should not be considered the primary focus. For projects involving significant participation of companies with experience in satellite development, all but one were a success and demonstrated the strength of the Cubesat for non-educational applications. It is estimated that at least 12 Cubesat missions could be considered to have demonstrated significant successful in-orbit operations for a sustained period. All Cubesats missions to date may be considered to have had technological objectives to some degree, be it the demonstration of devices and system architectures developed in-house, or demonstration of Non-Space-Rated (NSR) Commercial-Off-The-Shelf (COTS) component performance. Some Cubesats have also attempted to fulfill other mission objectives, although categorizing these accurately can be difficult

A simple Cubesat controller can be developed from a standard embedded platform such as the Arduino. The lack of radiation hardness can be balanced by the short on-orbit lifetime. The main drivers for a Cubesat flight computer are small size, small power consumption, wide functionality, and flexibility. In addition, a wide temperature range is desirable. The architecture should support a real time operating system, but, in the simplest case, a simple loop program with interrupt support can work.

Earth imaging is a common objective for a Cubesat mission, typically achieved using a CMOS camera without any complex lens systems. As a critical impediment to the development of a highly capable platform for mission operations, the testing and evaluation of novel approaches for increasing downlink data rate and reliability is also a common objective. While less common than Earth imaging, real science objectives are becoming increasingly popular as recognition (primarily by NASA) of Cubesat capabilities increase and collaborations between engineering and science groups emerge. Utility covers objectives not covered by the other categories and developed to handle a particular non-scientific demand.

Additional capabilities of proposed future missions either in planning or in development include: space weather monitoring, inflatable de-orbit devices, Earth imaging with optical lens, cosmic ray showers, shape memory alloys, star mapping, data relay, re-programmable computing, nano-meteorid dust, plasma probe, and multi-spectral remote sensing.

Cost reduction in these projects has been achieved through a number of mechanisms, some of which are unavailable to the conventional space industry. The lowest cost yet successful mission is reported to be estimated as under $100,000 (although the mission was not fitted with solar arrays). A typical cost for a university project varies considerably but a very approximate estimation might be from $50,000 to $150,000 for launch and $5-10,000. in parts cost per unit. Piggyback launches have been offered for free to Cubesats by launch vehicle operators and space agencies, negating the majority of launch cost.

Another important and related aspect in the design approach is that of modularity in a complete and integrated Cubesat life cycle, effectively representing a modular system of systems. The accelerated life cycle demonstrated consistently by small satellites, and harnessed by many Cubesat developers, can be further enhanced by the application of modularity to the complete life cycle. Cubesats are ideal teaching tools for aerospace engineering student , even if they are not going to fly.

Cubesat on - board computers

A simple Cubesat controller can be developed from a standard embedded platform such as the Arduino. The lack of radiation hardness can be balanced by the short on-orbit lifetime. The main drivers for a Cubesat flight computer are small size, small power consumption, wide functionality, and flexibility. In addition, a wide temperature range is desirable. The architecture should support a real time operating system, but, in the simplest case, a simple loop program with interrupt support can work. Both the Arduino and the Raspberry Pi, mentioned here, are based on the ARM architecture.

Arduino

The 32-bit implementation of the Arduino architecture is a strong candidate for Cubesat onboard computers. Many implementations feature a real-time clock, which is an add-on item in the Raspberry Pi architecture. A real time clock allows for the implementation of a real-time operating system. Cubesats with Arduinos have flown in orbit. The Arduino mini on the unit from Interorbital systems incorporates a current sensor to indicate a single event upset may have occurred due to radiation. The Arduino architecture has a relatively low tolerance to radiation damage (see, references, Violette).

There is actually a rad-hard Arduino architecture from Atmel, the AtmegaS128. It features 128 kBytes of flash, 4 kbytes of Eeprom, 4 kbytes of SRAM, 6 PWM channels, 1 analog compatator, 1 I2C interface, 1 SPI interface, 2 UARTS, 1 ADC, a real time clock, JTAG, and a watchdog timer. The device has 6 sleep modes. It is an 8-bit part, running on 3.3 volts, in a 64-lead ceramic package (CQFP). At this writing, there is a 16-week leadtime to get the part, which is priced over $600.

Edison

The Intel Edison board is an emerging competitor to the Arm based boards such as the Arduino and Pi. It uses Intel's x86 architecure. The actual computer module is the size of an SD card.

The second version, from 2014, is 35.5 x 25 mm, with a dual core 500 MHz Atom processor, and a 100 Mhz 32-bit Intel Quark core. The Quark cpu handles RTOS functions.

The Edison board supports vrious I/O options including GPIO, USB, SPI, I2C, and PWM. There is a Edison board which is compatible (in a hardware sense) with the Arduino Uno. The Intel Galileo line is a series of x86 architecture "Arduino's." It runs linux, and supports the Arduino "sketches" at the source level.

The Raspberry Pi

The Raspberry Pi is a small, inexpensive, single board computer based on the ARM architecture. It is targeted to the academic market. It uses the Broadcom BCM2835 system-on-a-chip, which has a 700 MHz ARM processor, a video GPU, and currently 512 M of RAM. It uses an SD card for storage. The Raspberry Pi runs the GNU/linux and FreeBSD operating systems. It was first sold in February 2012. Sales reached ½ million units by the Fall. Due to the open source nature of the software, Raspberry Pi applications and drivers can be downloaded from various sites. It requires a single power supply, and dissipates less than 5 watts. It has USB ports, and an Ethernet controller. It does not have a real-time clock, but one can easily be added. It outputs video in HDMI resolution, and supports audio output. I/O includes 8 general purpose I/O lines, UART, I2C bus, and SPI bus.

The Raspberry Pi design belongs to the Raspberry Pi Foundation in the UK, which was formed to promote the study of Computer Science. The Raspberry Pi is seen as the successor to the original BBC Microcomputer by Acorn, which resulted in the ARM processor. The unit has enough resources to host an operating system such as linux.

Although the Raspberry Pi is not designed to be Rad hard, it showed a surprisingly good radiation tolerance in tests (in references, see Violette). It continued to operate through a dose of 150 krad(Si), with only the loss of USB connectivity.

If you want guaranteed performance with radiation hardened hardware, it will cost more, but quite a few vendors are available. Here are a few examples.

The NanoMind A712D is an onboard computer for Cubesats. It uses as 32-bit ARM cpu, with 2 megabytes of RAM, and 8 megabytes of flash memory. It can also support a MicroSD flash card. It has a Can bus and a I^2C interface. It comes with an extensive software library and real time operating system. Special applications, such as attitude determination and control code are available. It is tolerant to temperatures form -40 to 85 degrees C, but is not completely rad-hard.

The CFC-300 from InnoFlight Inc. of San Diego is another example. It uses the Xilinx Zynq System-on-a-chip architecture. That provides both FPGA capability, and an Arm Cortex A-9 dual core cpu. It has 256 Megabytes of SDRAM, and 32 megabytes of flash. There are multiple synchronous serial interfaces. Daughter cards provide support for SpaceWire, Ethernet, RapidIO, RS-422, and thermistor inputs and heater drive outputs. It can be used with linux or VxWorks.

The Intrepid Cubesat OBC from Tyvak Uses a 400 MHz Atmel processor, and has 128 Mbytes of SDRAM, and 512 Mbytes of flash memory. It draws between 200-300 milliwatts. It includes a command and data handling system, and an onboard electrical power controller. It supports Ethernet, RS-232, USB, and the SPI and I²C interfaces. It includes a JTAG debugging interface. Similar to the Arduino, it supports 3-axis gyros, a 3-axis magnetometer, accelerometers, and a variety of i²c-interfaced sensors. The Microcontroller is an ARM architecture, with digital signal processing extensions. It has a built-in Image Sensor interface.

COVE is JPL's Xilinx Virtex-5 FPGA-based onboard processor for Cubesats. The FPGA is rad-hard. This high end machine provides sufficient power for onboard data processing, while providing a low power mode for periods where the number crunching is not needed. The FPGA can be reconfigured in flight. It has flown in space several times.

The Yaliny flight computer is based on the Microsemi Igloo-2 FPGA SOC. It is inherently SEU-immune. There is a soft processor core, implemented withing the FPGA. It has 8 megs of non-volatile, error-correcting memory, and 16 megs of static ram with error-correction. There is the ability to support 1 gigabyte of DDR SDRAM with error correction. It supports the 1553 bus, Ethernet, RS-485 quad pci-express busses, and usb (for debugging). The processor dissipates 2 watts nominally.

The proliferation of low cost and hobbyist grade Flight Computers can only have a positive effect on making the next generation of spacecraft smarter and cheaper.

At NASA and many National Labs, Cubesats have been a game-changer. The cost to develop, build, and test a concept or technology has gone down by orders of magnitude. This precursor technology has not only gone down in price, but the implementation process has been accelerated.

A recent NASA/GSFC Cubesat project, Dellingr, is set for launch as this book is being prepared. This will be a 6U (12" x 8" x 4") size. It was a one-year project to design, develop, test, and integrate the unit. It will be heading to the International Space Station. It is a Heliophysics payload, carrying an ion/neutral mass spectrometer. The design will be made available as Open Source after the mission is kicked off.

Another project was the NSF-funded Firefly mission, launched in November of 2013, and now returning good data on terrestrial Gamma ray flashes, These are interesting phenomena, involving high energy electrons generated by thunderstorms. Firefly uses a Pumpkin flight Motherboard for avionics, based on the Texas Instruments MSP430 chip. That unit is a 16-bit risc microcontroller architecture, The unit is ultra-low power, and mixed signal, supporting analog. It includes a real-time clock, and non-volatile FRAM memory.

The cpu on a Cubesat can be whatever the mission organization wishes to use. Popular architectures are the 8-bit and 32-bit Arduino embedded controllers, the PIC, and the PPM, pluggable process module, which uses an 8051. The Raspberry Pi is also applied to "PiSats." The author teaches at Capitol Technology University, which has cubesat classes, and several active cubesat projects.

Rad-Hard ARM

There are several Rad-Hard ARM microcontrollers available at this writing. There use either the M7 or M0 architecture. These are equivalent to the Arduino architectures in common use as microcontrollers.

RadHard ARM Cortex-M0

This unit is a microcontroller from Protec GmbH, a company with 30 years experience in rad-hard electronics, and a portfolio of processor and support parts. It provides a Cortex M0 cpu, operating at 50 Mhz, and using 3.3 volts. Memory includes 16k each of data and program memory. Error detection and correction is included. It can interface with up to 36 megabytes of external memory. It includes GPIO pins, that can also be used as interrupts. There are 32 general purpose counter-timers, and dual UARTS. There are dual SPI interfaces.

All internal registers are triple-modular redundant. It is hardened to a TID of 300 krad, and is latch-up immune to 100 MeV-cm^2/mg. It comes in a 1.3 x 1.3 inch, 188 pin package. Not a computational powerhouse, it is a capable controller.

SAMRH71

The SAMRH71 is a rad-hard-by-design microcontroller chip from Microchip, based on their commercial grade SAMv71. It is a 32-bit Cortex M7. The rad hard version includes Spacewire and MIL-STD-1553 I/O. The radiation performance is a LET of 62 MeV/CM^2 with an SEU greater than 20 and a TID of 100 Krad. This microcontroller operates up to 100 MHz. Besides the rad-hard part, a less-expensive radiation-tolerant part is also available. The part includes CAN and Ethernet interfaces.

VA10820

This chip, from Vorago, is based on the Cortex M0 architecture. It is 32 bits, rated beyond 300 krad, and is latch-up immune to 110 MeV-cm^2/mg. It includes 32k of data, and 128 k of program memory. For I/O, it includes dual UART's, dual I^{2}C's, and three SPI's. It comes in a 128 pin ceramic package. The memory, using

EDAC, is rated at fewer than 10^{-13} errors/bit-day. It implements EDAC, and TMR on critical functions. The similar PA32KAS offers 16k data and program data

High-Performance Spaceflight Computing Program

Looming on the horizon is a product from the ongoing AFSL/NASA Next Generation Space Processor (NGSP) Project. This will not be a rad-hard Arm-based microcontroller, but rather something similar to the Raspberry Pi architecture. It will have a 64-bit product, with 8 cores. It will be a capable number cruncher, and will support common open-source software, both operating systems and high-end applications. It is based on the ARM Cortex A53 architecture. This unit is superscalar, with dual units. It has an 8-stage pipeline, a floating point unit, hardware virtualization. and conditional branch prediction. Most instructions can be issued in pairs. It will be available as a licensable IP core.

The High Performance Spacecraft Computing Project (HPSC) is ongoing. The contract for development of the unit was let to the Boeing Company, in St. Louis. The contract value exceeds $26 million. The company is to develop the rad-hard computer based on the ARM architecture, multicore "chiplets, and associated software. Each chiplet has eight processor cores, and interfaces to memory and I/O resources. The architecture supports real-time, and parallel processing. The software environment is based on linux. Delivery of the computer will be by 2021.

There have been numerous space projects utilizing the ARM processor. To be used in a mission-critical application in space, the processor has to be insensitive to radiation damage. This involves both circuit-level and architectural (implementation) techniques for radiation hardening against both total dose and transient events, such as single event upsets (SEU's). These areas are fairly well understood, and techniques such as TMR (triple modular redundancy) and error detection and correction codes are employed. These techniques apply not only to the CPU, but also the memory and I/O circuitry as well.

Besides attitude determination and control, the onboard embedded system has a variety of housekeeping tasks to attend to.

Generally, there is a dedicated unit, sometimes referred to as the Command & Data Handler (C&DH) with interfaces with the spacecraft transmitters and receivers, the onboard data storage system, and the flight computer. The C&DH, itself a computer, is in charge of uplinked data (generally, commands), onboard data storage, and data transmission. The C&DH can forward received commands directly to various spacecraft components, or can hold them for later execution at a specified time. The C&DH has a direct connection with the science instrument(s) for that data stream. If the science instrument package has many units, there may be a separate science C&DH (SC&DH) that consolidates the sensed data, and hands it over to the C&DH for transmission to the ground. It is also common for the C&DH to hand over all commands related to science instruments to the IC&DH.

Strength in numbers

As a standard ARM architecture, the NGSP will support the use of standard, open source, operating systems such as linux, and applications. One relevant open source software is NASA/GSFC's Beowulf, which allows clustering. For example, a 64-node cluster computer, using the Pi architecture has already been built. The throughput is staggering. Additions to the original software allow for load leveling across the unit. The Beowulf cluster can be built from standard off-the-shelf commercial grade parts, with one rad-hard watchdog computer keeping tabs on all the compute units. It would also do trending across the cluster, and watch for pending problems that might be avoided with a timely reset.

Such as cluster computer could be utilized to support, in situ, a distributed space system, such as a swarm or constellation of Cubesats. These would be observing the same target from different points of view, or using different sensor types. The Intelligent Constellation Executive, or "mothership" would provide local management, control, and data processing for the swarm. This is a type of space-based sensor web, using multiple cooperating systems, managed locally.

The PIC

PIC is a family of Harvard architecture microcontrollers made by Microchip Technology, derived from the PIC1650 originally developed by General Instrument's Microelectronics Division. The name PIC initially referred to "Peripheral Interface Controller".
PICs are popular with both industrial developers and hobbyists alike due to their low cost, wide availability, large user base, extensive collection of application notes, availability of low cost or free development tools, and serial programming (and re-programming with flash memory) capability. Microchip announced on February 2008 the shipment of its six billionth PIC processor.

The PIC architecture is characterized by its multiple attributes, including separate code and data spaces (Harvard architecture) for devices other than PIC32, which has a Von Neumann architecture. It has a small number of fixed length instructions, with most instructions being single cycle execution (2 clock cycles, or 4 clock cycles in 8 bit models), with one delay cycle on branches and skips. There is One accumulator (W0), the use of which (as source operand) is implied (i.e. is not encoded in the opcode), All RAM locations function as registers as both source and/or destination of math and other functions. A hardware stack is used for storing return addresses. A fairly small amount of addressable data space is provided (typically 256 bytes), which can be extended through memory banking. The program counter is mapped into the data space and writable (this is used to implement indirect jumps).

Popular with cubesat makers is the PIC33, a 16 bit architecture. It is basically a PIC24F, with Digital Signal Processing capability, 128k flash, and a series of peripherals including ADC's and comm interfaces.

The Arduino is a simple open-source single-board microcontroller. The hardware consists of a simple open hardware design for the Arduino board with an 8-bit Atmel processor and on-board I/O support. The software support includes a standard compiler and a boot loader that runs on the board, along with numerous libraries of code.

The project began in Italy in 2005 to produce a device for implementing student-built design projects less expensively. By mid-2011, more than 300,000 Arduino boards had been shipped.

An Arduino board consists of an 8-bit Atmel AVR microcontroller or an Atmel 32-bit ARM. An important aspect of the Arduino is the standard way that connectors are arranged, allowing the CPU board to be connected to a variety of interchangeable add-on modules called *shields*. Shields allow for interfacing with sensors and actuators, as well as general I/O. Most boards include a 5-volt linear regulator and a 16 MHz crystal oscillator although some designs dispense with the on-board voltage regulator. An Arduino's microcontroller comes with a boot loader that simplifies uploading of programs to the on-chip flash memory.

Later variations of the Arduino architecture use a ARM 32 bit processor.

A simple Cubesat controller can be developed from a standard embedded platform such as the Arduino. The lack of radiation hardness can be balanced by the short on-orbit lifetime. The main drivers for a Cubesat flight computer are small size, small power consumption, wide functionality, and flexibility. In addition, a wide temperature range is desirable. The architecture should support a real time operating system.

The 32-bit implementation of the Arduino architecture is a strong candidate for Cubesat onboard computers. Many implementations feature a real-time clock, which is an add-on item in the Raspberry Pi architecture. A real time clock allows for the implementation of a real-time operating system. Cubesats with Arduinos have flown in orbit. The Arduino mini on the unit from Interorbital systems incorporates a current sensor to indicate a single event upset may have occurred due to radiation. The Arduino architecture has a relatively low tolerance to radiation damage. On the International Space Station, the dual Raspberry Pi B+ based AstroPi runs student -submitted software. The units are on the ISS LAN, and can be uploaded and downloaded from the ground. They make use of WiFi and have 32G micro SD cards. Raspbian is the operating system.

Although the standard Raspberry Pi is not designed to be Rad hard, it showed a surprisingly good radiation tolerance in tests. It continued to operate through a dose of 150 krad(Si), with only the loss of USB connectivity. Several commercial cubesat flight computers are based on the ARM architecture of the Pi. When the rad-hard P emerges, the games changes significantly.

The NanoMind A712D is an onboard computer for Cubesats. It uses a 32-bit ARM cpu, with 2 megabytes of RAM, and 8 megabytes of flash memory. It can also support a MicroSD flash card. It has a Can bus and a I^2C interface. It comes with an extensive software library and real time operating system. Special applications, such as attitude determination and control code are available. It is tolerant to temperatures form -40 to 85 degrees C, but is not completely rad-hard.

The UK Space agency kicked off a project in December of 2014 called Astro Pi. It was a competition for primary and secondary schools to come up with a project and associated code for a Cubesat. Two units were taken by British Astronaut Tim Peake to the International Space Station in December of 2015. Each has a camera (one for visible spectrum, one for infrared), and each has a magnetometer as well as temperature and humidity sensors. Each unit is standard, but is housed in a purpose built aluminum case.

The PiSat is a product of the Goddard Space Flight Center. It uses a Raspberry Pi flight controller, with a battery of sensors. The case is 3D printed. The project kicked off the 2014. The software is the GSFC Core Flight System modules.

Space Cube

The Space Cube Processor represents a family of reconfigurable architectures, using Xilinx Virtex-4 FPGA's with four integral PowerPC 405 450 MHz microprocessor cores. the SpaceCube was developed at NASA's Goddard Space Flight Center. The first SpaceCube into space was on the Hubble Servicing Mission 4, part of the Relative Navigation Sensors autonomous docking experiment. A subsequent mission (STS-129) carried a SpaceCube that was attached to the outside of the International Space Station, on the Naval Research Laboratory's MISSE7 experiment. SpaceCube is so-called because the packaging is a 4-inch cube. It uses less than 10 watts, and weighs less than four pounds. A unique stacking architecture is used for the mechanical and electrical inter-connection of the boards.

The follow-on SpaceCube's use the newer Virtex-5 architecture, which is available in a radiation hardened version. Previous versions used the commercial version, with a "Rad hard by Architecture: approach. the four integral processors provide a quad-redundant system, and a small, inherently radiation-hard processor serves as the voting device.

The FPGA in the SpaceCube has four instantiated PowerPC cpus, and the ability to instantiate more in the "sea of logic" that makes up the bulk of the device. The Xilinx "Microblaze" architecture is popular, and the chip can easily hold 16 of these devices, with an associated interconnect mechanism. The device can be reprogrammed or reconfigured in orbit.

The Xilinx FPGA's in non-radiation hardened versions, have flown on a variety of space missions, including the Australian FEDSAT mission, the Spirit and Opportunity Rovers on Mars, the MARS 2003 Lander and Rover, the Mars Science Laboratory, the Venus Express, TacSat-2, and others. Mitigation techniques for radiation effects include combinations of Triple Modular Redundancy (TMR), Error Detection and Correction (EDAC) circuitry, and memory scrubbing.

Glossary

1's complement – a binary number representation scheme for negative values.

2's complement – another binary number representation scheme for negative values.

2-wire – twisted pair wire channel for full duplex communications. Still needs a common ground.

Accumulator – a register to hold numeric values during and after an operation.

ACM – Association for Computing Machinery; professional organization.

ALU – arithmetic logic unit.

Analog – concerned with continuous values.

AND – logical operation on data. Output is true, if and only if both inputs are true

ANSI – American National Standards Institute

Arduino – open source, single board microcontroller using an Atmel AVR (8-bit RISC) CPU.

ASCII - American Standard Code for Information Interchange, a 7-bit code; developed for teleprinters.

ASIC – application specific integrated circuit.

Assembly language – low level programming language specific to a particular ISA.

Async – asynchronous; using different clocks.

Baud – symbol rate; may or may not be the same as bit rate.

Baudot – a five-bit code used with teleprinters.

BCD – binary coded decimal. 4-bit entity used to represent 10 different decimal digits; with 6 spare states.

Big-endian – data format with the most significant bit or byte at the lowest address, or transmitted first.

Binary – using base 2 arithmetic for number representation.

BIST – built-in self test.

Bit – smallest unit of digital information; two states.

Blackbox – functional device with inputs and outputs, but no detail on the internal workings.

Boolean – a data type with two values; an operation on these data types; named after George Boole, mid-19th century inventor of Boolean algebra.

Borrow – mathematical operation when a digit become smaller than limit and the deficiency is taken from the next digit to the left.

Buffer – a temporary holding location for data.

Bug – an error in a program or device.

Bus – data channel, communication pathway for data transfer.

Byte – ordered collection of 8 bits; values from 0-255

Cache – faster and smaller intermediate memory between the processor and main memory.

CADC – Central Air Data Computer

Carry – arithmetic result, when a digit is larger than a limit and the extra is moved to the left.

CAS – column address strobe (in DRAM refreshing)

Chip – integrated circuit component.

Clock – periodic timing signal to control and synchronize operations.

CMOS – complementary metal oxide semiconductor; a technology using both positive and negative semiconductors to achieve low power operation.

Complement – in binary logic, the opposite state.

Control Flow – computer architecture involving directed flow through the program; data dependent paths are allowed.

Coprocessor – another processor to supplement the operations of the main processor. Used for floating point, video, etc. Usually relies on the main processor for instruction fetch; and control.

Core – early non-volatile memory technology based on ferromagnetic toroids.

Cots – commercial, off-the-shelf.

CPU – central processing unit.

DCE – data communications equipment; interface to the network.

DEMUX – demultiplex.

Digital – using discrete values for representation of states or numbers.

DMA - direct memory access (to/from memory, for I/O devices).

Double word – two words; if word = 8 bits, double word = 16-bits.

Dram – dynamic random access memory.

Drum memory – obsolete storage media using large cylindrical magnetic media.

DTE – data terminal equipment; communicates with the DCE to get to the network.

DTL – diode-transistor logic.

EDAC – error detection and correction circuitry.

EIA – Electronics Industry Association.

Embedded system – a computer systems with limited human interfaces and performing specific tasks. Usually part of a larger system.

Epitaxial – in semiconductors, having a crystalline overlayer with a well-defined orientation.

Eprom – erasable programmable read-only memory.

EEprom – electrically erasable read-only memory.

Exception – interrupt due to internal events, such as overflow.

Fail-safe – a system designed to do no harm in the event of failure.

FET – field effect transistor.

Fetch/execute cycle – basic operating cycle of a computer; fetch the instruction, execute the instruction.

Firmware – code contained in a non-volatile memory.

Fixed point – computer numeric format with a fixed number of digits or bits, and a fixed radix point. Integers.

Flag – a binary indicator.

Flip-flop – a circuit with two stable states; ideal for binary.

Floating point – computer numeric format for real numbers; has significant digits and an exponent.

FPGA – field programmable gate array.

FPU – floating point unit, an ALU for floating point numbers.

Full duplex – communication in both directions simultaneously.

Gate – a circuit to implement a logic function; can have multiple inputs, but a single output.

Glue logic – some simple logic to interface two devices, for level shifting or simple functions.

Gray – unit of radiation does equal to 100 rad.

Half-duplex – communications in two directions, but not simultaneously.

Handshake – co-ordination mechanism.

Harvard architecture – memory storage scheme with separate instructions and data.

Hexadecimal – base 16 number representation.

Hexadecimal point – radix point that separates integer from fractional values of hexadecimal numbers.

HP – Hewlett-Packard Company. Instrumentation and computers.

IEEE – Institute of Electrical and Electronic Engineers. Professional organization and standards body.

IEEE-754 – standard for floating point representation and operations.

I^2L – integrated injection logic, a bipolar technology.

Index register – register to hold addresses.

Infinity - the largest number that can be represented in the number system.

Integer – the natural numbers, zero, and the negatives of the natural numbers.

Interrupt – an asynchronous event to signal a need for attention (example: the phone rings).

Interrupt vector – entry in a table pointing to an interrupt service routine; indexed by interrupt number.

I/O – Input-output from the computer to external devices, or a user interface.

IP – intellectual property; also internet protocol.

IP core – IP describing a chip design that can be licensed to be used in an FPGA or ASIC.

ISA – instruction set architecture, the software description of the computer.

ISO – International Standards Organization.

ISR – interrupt service routine, a subroutine that handles a particular interrupt event.

JTAG – Joint Test Action Group; industry group that lead to IEEE 1149.1, Standard Test Access Port and Boundary-Scan Architecture.

Junction – in semiconductors, the boundary interface of the n-type and p-type material.

Kilo – a prefix for 10^3 or 2^{10}

Latency – time delay.

Little-endian – data format with the least significant bit or byte at the highest address, or transmitted last.

Logic operation – generally, negate, AND, OR, XOR, and their inverses.

LSB – least significant bit or byte.

Machine language – native code for a particular computer hardware.

Mainframe – a computer you can't lift.

Mantissa – significant digits (as opposed to the exponent) of a floating point value.

Master-slave – control process with one element in charge. Master status may be exchanged among elements.

Math operation – generally, add, subtract, multiply, divide.

Mega - 10^6 or 2^{20}

MeV – million electron volts.

Microcode – hardware level data structures to translate machine instructions into sequences of circuit level operations.

Microcontroller – microprocessor with included memory and/or I/O.

Microprocessor – a monolithic CPU on a chip.

Microprogramming – modifying the microcode,

Minicomputer – smaller than a mainframe, larger than a pc.

MIPS – millions of instructions per second; sometimes used as a measure of throughput.

Modem – modulator/demodulator; digital communications interface for analog channels.

MSB – most significant bit or byte.

Multiplex – combining signals on a communication channel by sampling.

Mux - multiplex

NAN – not-a-number; invalid bit pattern.

NAND – negated (or inverse) AND function.

NASA – National Aeronautics and Space Administration.

NDA – non-disclosure agreement; legal agreement protecting IP.

Negate – logical operation on data; changes the state.

Nibble – 4 bits, ½ byte.

NIST – National Institute of Standards and Technology (US), previously, National Bureau of Standards.

NMI – non-maskable interrupt; cannot be ignored by the software.

NOR – negated (or inverse) OR function

Normalized number – in the proper format for floating point representation.

NRE – non-recurring engineering; one-time costs for a project.

NSSC – NASA Standard Spacecraft Computer.

Null modem – acting as two modems, wired back to back. Artifact of the RS-232 standard.

NVM – non-volatile memory.

Nxor – logical operation on data; negated XOR.

Nyquist rate – in communications, the minimum sampling rate, equal to twice the highest frequency in the signal.

Octal – base 8 number.

Off-the-shelf – commercially available; not custom.

Opcode – part of a machine language instruction that specifies the operation to be performed.

OR – logical operation on data; output is true if either or both inputs are true.

Overflow - the result of an arithmetic operation exceeds the capacity of the destination.

Paradigm – a pattern or model

Paradigm shift – a change from one paradigm to another. Disruptive or evolutionary.

Parallel – multiple operations or communication proceeding simultaneously.

Parity – an error detecting mechanism involving an extra check bit in the word.

PC – personal computer, politically correct, program counter.

PCB – printed circuit board.

PIC – a microcontroller from Microchip Technology.

Pinout – mapping of signals to I/O pins of a device.

PLC – Programmable logic controller, embedded device for automation.

PLD– programmable logic device; generic gate-level part that can be programmed for a function.

PROM – programmable read-only memory.

Quad word – four words. If word = 16-bits, quad word is 64 bits.

Queue – first in, first out data buffer structure; hardware of software.

Rad – unit of absorbed radiation dose; 100 ergs per gram; also, radian, angular measurement.

Radix point – separates integer and fractional parts of a real number.

RAM – random access memory; any item can be access in the same time as any other.

RAS – Row address strobe, in dram refresh.

Register – temporary storage location for a data item.

Reset – signal and process that returns the hardware to a known, defined state.

RISC – reduced instruction set computer.

ROM – read only memory.

Real-time – system that responds to events in a predictable, bounded time.

RS-232 – EIA telecommunications standard (1962), serial with handshake.

RTL – register transfer level, description of logic circuit.

SAM – sequential access memory, like a magnetic tape.

Self-modifying code – computer code that modifies itself as it run; hard to debug

Semiconductor – material with electrical characteristics between conductors and insulators; basis of current technology processor and memory devices.

Semaphore –signaling element among processes.

Serial – bit by bit.

Seu – single event upset; radiation induced upset in a device.

Shift – move one bit position to the left or right in a word.

Sign-magnitude – number representation with a specific sign bit.

Signed number – representation with a value and a numeric sign.

SOC – system on chip.

SOS – Silicon on Sapphire, an inherently radiation tolerant (yet, expensive) fabrication.

Software – set of instructions and data to tell a computer what to do.

SRAM – static random access memory.

Stack – first in, last out data structure. Can be hardware or software.

Stack pointer – a reference pointer to the top of the stack.

State machine – model of sequential processes.

Synchronous – using the same clock to coordinate operations.

System – a collection of interacting elements and relationships with a specific behavior.

Test-and-set – coordination mechanism for multiple processes that allows reading to a location and writing it in a non-interruptible manner.

TCP/IP – transmission control protocol/internet protocol; layered set of protocols for networks.

TMR – Triple Modular Redundancy; an error control mechanism using redundant components.

Transceiver – receiver and transmitter in one box.

TRAP – exception or fault handling mechanism in a computer; an operating system component.

Triplicate – using three copies (of hardware, software, messaging, power supplies, etc.). for redundancy and error control.

Truncate – discard. Cutoff, make shorter.

TTL – transistor-transistor logic in digital integrated circuits. (1963)

Tri-state – logic device with 2 state, plus a high-impedance state

UART – universal asynchronous receiver-transmitter. Parallel-to-serial; serial-to parallel device with handshaking.

USART – universal synchronous (or) asynchronous receiver/transmitter.

Underflow – the result of an arithmetic operation is smaller than the smallest representable number.

USAF – United States Air Force.

Unsigned number – a number without a numeric sign.

Vector – single dimensional array of values.

VHDL- very high level description language; a language to describe integrated circuits and asic/ fpga's.

Via – vertical conducting pathway through an insulating layer in a semiconductor.

Von Neumann, John, a computer pioneer and mathematician; realized that computer instructions are data.

Watchdog – hardware/software function to sanity check the hardware, software, and process; applies corrective action if a fault is detected; fail-safe mechanism.

Wiki – the Hawaiian word for "quick." Refers to a collaborative content website.

Word – a collection of bits of any size; does not have to be a power of two.

Write-only – of no interest.

XOR – exclusive OR; either but not both.

Zero address – architecture using implicit addressing, like a stack.

Bibliography

Alkalai, Leon "An Overview of Flight Computer Technologies for Future NASA Space Exploration Missions," Acta Astronautica, Volume 52, Issues 9–12, May–June 2003, Pages 857–867.

Cress, John D.; Mantooth, H. Alan; Extreme Environment Electronics, 2012, CRC Press, 1st ed, ISBN-1439874301.

DeCoursey, R.; Melton, Ryan; Estes, Robert R. Jr. "Sensors, Systems, and Next-Generation Satellites X," Proceedings of the SPIE, Vol. 6361 pp 63611m (2006).

Deese, Samuel G. "Application of Microprocessors to Interplanetary Spacecraft Data Systems," February, 1980, NASA/JPL.

Sergio De Florio; Eberhard Gill; Simone D'Amicoand; Andreas Grillenberger "PERFORMANCE COMPARISON OF MICROPROCESSORS FOR SPACE-BASED NAVIGATION APPLICATIONS,"
http://www.lr.tudelft.nl/fileadmin/Faculteit/LR/Organisatie/Afdelin gen_en_Leerstoelen/Afdeling_SpE/Space_Systems_Eng./Publicati ons/2009/doc/

Domse, Niveditha; Kumar, Kris; Murthy, K. N. Balasubramanya; "64 bit Computer Architectures for Space Applications – A study," World Academy of Science, Engineering and Technology, Vol 3 2009-03-28.

Dunford, C.M.; Thompson, J.A.; Yearby, *K.H.i* "A Transputer-based Instrument for the ESA/NASA Cluster Mission", *Concurrency Practice and Experience,* Aug 1991 v 3 n 4 p 293.

Dynex Semiconductor, MA31750, High Performance MIL-STD-1750 Microprocessor, January 2000, DS3748-8.0.

Figueiredo, Marco; Stakem, Patrick H.; Flatley, Thomas P.; Hines,

Tonjua M. "An Integrated Architecture for Onboard Spacecraft," IEEE Computer, June 1999, Document 19990063637 (see http://airex.tksc.jaxa.jp/pl/dr/19990063637/en).

Fortescue, Peter and Stark, John *Spacecraft System Engineering*, 2nd ed, Wiley, 1995, ISBN 0-471-95220-6.

Gaisler, Jiri, "A Portable and Fault-Tolerant Microprocessor Based on the SPARC V8
Architecture," http://www.gaisler.com/doc/dsn2002-3.pdf

Ghahroodi, Massoud M.; Ozer, Emre; Bull, David "SEU and SET-tolerant ARM Cortex-R4 CPU for Space and Avionics Applications," Southhampton University and ARM, Ltd. http://www.median-project.eu/wp-content/uploads/median2013_submission_5.pdf

Harland, David M. and Lorenz, Ralph D. Space Systems Failures, Springer Praxis, 2005, ISBN 0-387-21519-0.

Khaddaj, S.A.; Al-Bahadili, H.; Goddard, A.J.H.; "The Solution of Radiation Engineering Problems on a Transputer-based System", Concurrency Practice and Experience, Aug 1991 v 3 n 4 p 423.

Khan, Mohammad Ziaullah and Trout, Joseph G. "Detection of Upset Induced Errors in Microprocessors," 1989, IEEE, 8th Annual International Phoenix Conference on Computers and Communications, ISN 0896-582X, IEEE Computer Society 1981.

Kin, E. E. "Total Dose Testing of Several Types of MOS Microprocessors," IEEE T. Nuclear Science, Vol NS-25, No. 6, Oct. 1978.

Levenson, Nancy G. *Safeware, System Safety and Computers*, 1995, Addison Wesley, ISBN 0-201-11972-2

Marshall, Joseph R.; Stanley, Daniel; Robertson, Jeffrey E. "Matching Processor Performance to Mission Application Needs," AIAA 2011-1620.

Pouponnot, Andre L.R., "A Giga Instruction Architecture (GIGA) for the Future ESA Microprocessor based on the LEON3 IP core," ESA ESTEC DATA Systems In Aerospace conference Berlin, Germany, ESA SP360-July 2006.

Pouponnot, Andre L.R., "ESA Microprocessors," ESA ESTEC, Presentation May 2006 at ISD Noordwijk.

Shatom, E. "THE INPUT OUTPUT UNIT FOR THE ATTITUDE AND ARTICULATION CONTROL SUBSYSTEM ON THE CASSINI SPACECRAFT," JPL, IEEE, Digital Avionics Systems Conference, 1995., 14th DASC, 5-9 Nov 1995 , ISBN 0-7803-3050-1.

Silicon Space Technology showcases their Radiation Hardened SRAM's, ARM® Cortex® M0 Processor and new Sapphire Development Kit at the Space Tech Expo. (Press Release) http://www.siliconspacetech.com/search/node/arm

Sorin, Daniel J. and Ozev, Sule, "Fault Tolerant Microprocessors for Space Missions," Duke University.

Stakem, Patrick H. "One Step Forward - Three Steps Backup, computing in the U.S. Space Program," Sept 1981, BYTE Magazine, pp 112-144.

Stakem, Patrick H. *The History of Spacecraft Computers from the V-2 to the Space Station*, 2011, PRB publishing, ASIN B004L626U6.

Stakem, Patrick H. "The Applications of Computers and Microprocessors Onboard Spacecraft, NASA/GSFC, 1980.

Stakem, Patrick H. *Flight Linux Project Target Architecture Technical Report*, NASA-GSFC, 6/2000.

Tomayko, James "Computers in Spaceflight, The NASA Experience," 1987.

http://history.nasa.gov/computers/contents.html

Wilson, Kevin T. Analysis of 32-bit Processors for Space system Applications, Feb. 2, 1994, innovative systems & technologies corporation (sic).

RISC-V

Acle, Julio Perez, et al "Implementing a safe embedded computing system in SRAM-based FPGAs using IP cores: A case study based on the Altera NIOS-II soft processor," 2011 IEEE Second Latin American Symposium on Circuits and Systems (LASCAS), Bogata, Columbia, Feb. 2011, IEEE Xplore 15 April 2011.

Asanovic, Krste, *"RISC-V: An Open Standard for SoCs,"2015, avail:* https://www.eetimes.com/author.asp? section_id=36&_mc=RSS_EET_EDT&doc_id=1323406&page_n umber=2.

Asanovic, Krste, et al *The Rocket Chip Generator*, UC Berkeley, avail: https://www2.eecs.berkeley.edu/Pubs/TechRpts/2016/EECS-2016-17.pdf

Blokdyk, Gerardus *RISC-V a Clear and Concise Reference,* 2018, ISBN-0655348662.

Goodman, James; Miller, Karen *A Programmer's View of Computer Architecture: With Assembly Language Examples from the MIPS RISC Architecture*, Oxford University Press, Preliminary ed., 1993, ISBN 0030972191.

Lee, Yunsup RISC-V "Rocket Chip" SoC Generator in Chisel, High-Performance Computer Architecture (HPCA), 2015. avail: http://darksilicon.org/hpca/

Patterson, David A., Hennessy, John L. *Computer Organization and Design, RISC-V Edition: The Hardware Software Interface* (The Morgan Kaufmann Series in Computer Architecture and Design), 1st Edition, 2917, ASIN-B0714LM21Z.

Patterson, David, Waterman, Andrew *The RISC-V Reader: An Open Architecture Atlas,* 2017, ISBN-0999249118.

Straka, Bartholomew F. "Implementing a Microcontroller Watchdog with a Field Programmable Gate Array (FPGA)", 2013, JSC. Avail:
https://ntrs.nasa.gov/archive/nasa/casi.ntrs.nasa.gov/20130013486.pdf

Waterman, A., K. Asanovi´c, K. (Eds.), *The RISC-V Instruction Set Manual, Volume I: User-Level ISA,* Version 2.2, May 2017. Avail: https://riscv.org/specifications/

Waterman, Andrw, et al The RISC-V Instruction Set Manual Volume II: Privileged Architecture, Version 1.10, avail: https://riscv.org/specifications/privileged-isa/

Resources

http://www.esa.int/Our_Activities/Space_Engineering_Technology/Onboard_Computer_and_Data_Handling/Onboard_Computer_and_Data_Handling2

http://legacy.cleanscape.net/stdprod/xtc1750a/resources/index.html

http://sd-www.jhuapl.edu/MSX/fact/MIL-STD-1750AAV.pdf

http://www.everyspec.com/MIL-STD/MIL-STD+%281700+-+1799%29/

http://www.ibm.com/developerworks/library/pa-microhist.html

Sahu, Kusum *Instructions for EEE Parts Selection, Screening, Qualification, and Derating,* April 2008, NASA/TP-2003-212242. nepp.**nasa**.gov/docuploads/FFB52B88-36AE.../**EEE-INST-002**_add1.pdf_

The Indian Mars Orbiter Mission:
http://www.spaceflight101.com/mars-orbiter-mission.html

Off-the-Shelf Space Processors, Briefing for NASA Langley Research Center, April 19, 1993, IBM Federal Systems, Manassas Laboratory.

wikipedia, various. Material from Wikipedia (www.wikipedia.org) is used under the conditions of the Creative commons Attribution-ShareAlike #.0 Unported License.
http://creativecommons.org/licenses/by-sa/3,0

https://riscv.org

RISCV Software Ecosystem, avail - https://riscv.org/wp-content/uploads/2015/02/riscv-software-toolchain-tutorial-hpca2015.pdf

The RISC-V Instruction Set Manual Volume II: Privileged Architecture Version 1.10, May 2017.Avail: https://riscv.org/specifications/

CADC

http://firstmicroprocessor.com/documents/ap1-26-97.pdf

8085

http://klabs.org/DEI/Processor/8085/index.htm

8051

http://klabs.org/DEI/Processor/8051/index.htm

http://klabs.org/DEI/Processor/87c51/index.htm

RTX 2010

Perschy, James A. "Command and Data Handling Processor," JHU/APL. (NERA and ACE missions, Harris RTX2010.

68000

Sawat Tantiphanwadi, Sawat *Spacecraft Computers on the SeaStar Satellite,* Orbital Sciences Corporation, 13th AIAA/USU Conference on Small Satellites, SSC99-XII-6.

80386/80387

80386 Programmer's Reference Manual, Intel, 1987, ISBN 1-55512-057-1 order 231917-001.

80386 Hardware Reference Manual, Intel, 1987, ISBN 1-55512-069-5, order 231732-002.

80387 Programmer's Reference Manual, Intel, 1987, ISBN 1-55512-057-1, order 231917-001.

80386 Technical Reference, Strauss, Brady Books, 1987, ISBN 0-13-246893-x.

Co-Processor, NASA Facts, NF-193, June 1993.

Radiation Hardened 80386RP High Speed CMOS 32-bit Microprocessor for Space Applications, SAIC.

Grim, Clifton *IBM FSD Houston 80386 Space Processor DMS Software Architecture Overview*, JSC Houston, Jan. 1988.

Moore, R. C. *Radiation Immunity of the 80386 Chipset*, SEE-96-0002, June 6, 1996.

Sharma, Ashok K. and Sahu, Kusum *Radiation Report on MQ80386-20 Microprocessors*, NASA/GSFC, Parts Technology Report 30582, July 1993.

Moran, Amh K and LaBel, Kenneth *A. Single Event Effect Test Report on the Intel 80386 Microprocessor, 80387 Coprocessor, and 82380 Integrated Peripheral tested 2/20-21/96*, March 7, 1996, NASA/GSFC, b022196.

LaBel, Ken Stassinopoulos, E. G. Brucker G. J. and Stauffer, C. A. "SEU Tests of a 80386 Based Flight Computer/Data-Handling System and of Discrete PROM and EEPROM Devices, and SEL Tests of Discrete 80386, 80387, PROM, EEPROM, and ASICS, NASA/GSFC.

<u>80486</u>

i486 Microprocessor, Intel Corp, order 240440-001, 1989

Hubble Space Telescope Servicing Mission 3A, New Advanced Computer, NASA/GSFC, FS-1999-06-009-GSFC.

Johnson, Donald R. McGraw, R. J. "Total Dose Test Report on the Intel 80486DX2-66 Microprocessor tested 8/29-9/9/95," Sept. 28, 1995, NASA/GSFC, td80486.

<u>Thor</u>

Rad Hard Thor Microprocessor Description, Saab Ericsson Space, P-TOR-NOT-0004-SE, Jan 1999.

SPARC

"SPARC At the Heart of the New Machine", Michael Slater, SunWorld, Fall 1992, P. 21-29.

"Sparc Takes off", High Performance Systems, June 1989.

"NASA gets a glimpse of 200 Mhz SPARC", EETimes, Feb. 22, 1993, P. 4.

Agrawal, A.; Garner, R. B.; "SPARC: A scalable processor architecture", Future Generations Computer Systems: FGCS, APR 01 1992 v 7 n 2 / 3 Page: 303.

"Sparc Gets Smaller Still", Computer Design, SEP 01 1991 v 30 n 12 Page:136.

LEON

Clarke, Peter "European Space Agency Launches Free Sparc-like Core," EE Times, 03/06/2000.

Clarke, Peter "Free Sparc Processor Developer Goes Commercial," Silicon Strategies, EEtimes , 02/24/2005.

D&R Industry Articles, Successful Use of an Open Source Processor in a Commercial ASIC

"Next Generation Multipurpose Microprocessor", J. Andersson, J. Gaisler, R. Weigand, Data Systems In Aerospace 2010, (DASIA2010), 2010.

Gaisler Research, Press release of the LEON4 processor

European Space Agency, LEON2FT

Aeroflex Gaisler, SOC Library

ESA Microelectronics, system-on-chip development

Gaisler Research, LEON3 processor characteristics

European Space Agency IP Cores Library LEON-2 FT page

Gaisler Research, LEON3FT-RTAX Fault-tolerant Processor
Gaisler Research, Press release of the LEON4 processor
http://klabs.org/DEI/Processor/sparc/index.htm

Pouponnot, A. L. R. "Principles of Radiation Hardening by
Design" The Case of Leon," Atelier Technicstome, Nov. 20,
2002.q

ERC 32

http://klabs.org/DEI/Processor/sparc/ERC32/ERC32_docs.htm

Gaisler, J. and Schmitt, J. "Development of a 32-bit
Microprocessor System," ESTEC, March 1995, Preparing for the
Future, Vol. 5 no 1.

Gutiérrez, Cristina Calzadilla "Microprocesadores aplicados a
sistemas espaciales," Microprocesadores para comunicaciones5
ETSIT.

MIPS

"MIPS RISC Architecture", Gerry Kane, Prentice Hall, 1988,
ISBN 0-13-584293-X.

"System Design Using the MIPS R3000/3010 RISC Chipset",
MIPS, IEEE Micro, 1989.

"The MIPS R3010 Floating Point Coprocessor", Rowen, Johnson, and Ries, IEEE Micro, June 1988.

LR3010/LR3010A MIPS Floating-Point Accelerator, User's Manual, LSI Logic.

Weiss, Ray; "Third-generation RISC processors", <u>EDN</u>, MAR 30 1992 v 37 n 7 Page: 96.

Cmelik, Robert F.; Ditzel, David R.; Kelly, Edmund J.; "An Analysis of SPARC and MIPS Instruction Set Utilization on the SPEC Benchmarks", <u>Sigplan notices</u>, APR 01 1991 v 26 n 4 Page: 290.

Bennett, C.; et al. (2003a). "The Microwave Anisotrophy Probe (MAP) Mission," Astrophysical Journal, 583: 1–23.

Vail, D. Estimating the On-Orbit Single Event Upset Behavior of a MIPS R3000 Microprocessor, Feb 1991, Harris Corporation.

<u>Mongoose</u>

http://klabs.org/DEI/Processor/Mongoose/index.htm

Mongoose-V 32-bit MIPS Microprocessor Architecture Description, Jan. 30, 1997 (Rev. 1.3) Synova www.synova.com

Smith, Brian S. *Mongoose ASIC Microcontroller Programming Guide,* September 1993, NASA/GSFC, NASA Reference publication 1319.

<u>Power-PC</u>

"IBM RISC System/6000 Technology", IBM Corp., 1990, SA23-2619

Oehler, Richard R.; Blasgen, Michael W.; "IBM RISC System/6000: Architecture and Performance", IEEE Micro, 1991 v 11 n 3 Page: 14

Technical summary PowerPC 601 RISC Microprocessor, Motorola, 4/93

PowerPC 601 RISC Microprocessor User's Manual, 1993.

Motorola PowerPC 750 and PowerPC 740 Microprocessors, MPC750FACT/D, Rev. 4, Motorola.1999.

MPC740 RISC Microprocessor Technical Summary, MPC750/D, 1997, Motorola.

RAD6000

RAD6000 Processor for Spaceborne Applications, June 1993, IBM Federal systems.

RHPPC

Brown, Gary "Radiation Hardened PowerPC 603e-based single board computer". *2001 IEEE Aerospace Conference Proceedings.* Big Sky, MT: IEEE, March 10-17, 2001. pp.2249–2261.

Lintz, J.P. "Single event effects hardening and characterization of Honeywell's RHPPC integrated circuit". *2003 IEEE Radiation Effects Data Workshop Record.* Monterey, CA: IEEE, (July 21-25, 2003) pp.156–164.

RAD-750

Berger,R.; Bayles, D.; Brown, R.; Doyle, S.; A. Kazemzadeh, K. Knowles, D. Moser, J. Rodgers, B. Saari, and D. Stanley The RAD750 - A Radiation Hardened PowerPC Processor for High Performance Spaceborne Applications; BAE Systems, Manassas,

VA Basil Grant LTS Corporation, Manassas, VA, IEEE Aerospace Conference, 2001.

Nguyen, Q., Yuknis, W., Pursley, S., Haghani, N., Albaijes, D.Haddad, O. "A High Performance Command and Data Handling System for NASA's Lunar Reconnaissance Orbiter," AIAA, 7/29/08.

RAD750Microprocessor Datasheet, Ver. 1.1, August 2000, Lockheed Martin Space Electronics & Communications Systems.

Transputer

Ciecior, et al, "A Transputer Based On-Board Data Handling system for Small Satellites," AIAA-93-4467-CP.

Cotarelo, Maria del Mar Lopez, "Proton Induced Single Event Upsets on Inmos T800, 21 March 1990, ESTEC.

Stakem, Patrick H. *The Hardware and Software Architecture of the Transputer,* PRRB Publishing, 2011, ASIN B004L626U6.

Thompson, J. A. and Hancock, B. K. "Report on the Suitability of the Inmos T222 and C011 for use in the Cluster mission radiation environment," Feb. 7, 1990.

Transputer Reference Manual, Inmos, Prentice Hall, 1988 ISBN 0-13-929001-X

The Military and Space Transputer Databook, 1990, Inmos.

An Initial Radiation Assessment of the Inmos IMS T414BG Transputer for Use in Space Projects, TR-86/157, Smith Associates, LTD. 10 Oct. 1986.

Report on Radiation Tolerance Testing of T425 Transputer, SIL/TR00209, 9 Feb 1990, Satellites International Ltd.

Spacecube

Curiel, Alex da Silva, Davies, Phil, and Bake, Adam, Underwood, Dr. Craig, and Vladimirova, Dr. Tanya; Towards Spacecraft-on-a-Chip, Surrey Space Technology.

Jones, Dr. Robert L. and Hodson, Dr. Robert F. "A Roadmap for the Development of Reconfigurable Computing for Space," Version 2.0, March 23, 2007, NASA-Langley Research Center.

Seagrave, Dorian Seagrave, Gordon, Godfrey, John Lin, Michael SpaceCube: A Reconfigurable Processing Platform For Space, 2008, MAPLD Proceedings.

Tiny FPGA-based Computer Accelerates Space Exploration, Xilinx Corp., Xcell Journal, Second quarter 2009.

SpaceCube to Debut in flight Demonstration: Hybrid Computer to Fly on Hubble Servicing Mission, NASA/GSFC, Office of the Chief   Technologist, http://gsfctechnology.gsfc.nasa.giov/SpaceCube.htm .

Radiation Effects

Holmes-Siedle, A. G. and Adams, L. *Handbook of Radiation Effects*, 2002, Oxford University Press, ISBN 0-19-850733-X.

Messenger, G. C. *The Effects of Radiation on Electronic Systems*, 2014, Springer, ISBN- 9401753571.

Maurer, Richard H.; Fraeman, Martin E.; Martin, Mark H.; Roth, David R. *Harsh Environments: Space Radiation Environment, Effects, and Mitigation,*
techdigest.jhuapl.edu/TD/td2801/Maurer.pdf

If you enjoyed this book, you might also be interested in some of these.

Stakem, Patrick H. *16-bit Microprocessors, History and Architecture*, 2013 PRRB Publishing, ISBN-1520210922.

Stakem, Patrick H. *4- and 8-bit Microprocessors, Architecture and History*, 2013, PRRB Publishing, ISBN-152021572X,

Stakem, Patrick H. *Apollo's Computers,* 2014, PRRB Publishing, ISBN-1520215800.

Stakem, Patrick H. *The Architecture and Applications of the ARM Microprocessors,* 2013, PRRB Publishing, ISBN-1520215843.

Stakem, Patrick H. *Earth Rovers: for Exploration and Environmental Monitoring,* 2014, PRRB Publishing, ISBN-152021586X.

Stakem, Patrick H. *Embedded Computer Systems, Volume 1, Introduction and Architecture*, 2013, PRRB Publishing, ISBN-1520215959.

Stakem, Patrick H. *The History of Spacecraft Computers from the V-2 to the Space Station*, 2013, PRRB Publishing, ISBN-1520216181.

Stakem, Patrick H. *Floating Point Computation*, 2013, PRRB Publishing, ISBN-152021619X.

Stakem, Patrick H. *Architecture of Massively Parallel Microprocessor Systems*, 2011, PRRB Publishing, ISBN-1520250061.

Stakem, Patrick H. *Multicore Computer Architecture,* 2014, PRRB Publishing, ISBN-1520241372.

Stakem, Patrick H. *Personal Robots*, 2014, PRRB Publishing, ISBN-1520216254.

Stakem, Patrick H. *RISC Microprocessors, History and Overview,* 2013, PRRB Publishing, ISBN-1520216289.

Stakem, Patrick H. *Robots and Telerobots in Space Applications*, 2011, PRRB Publishing, ISBN-1520210361.

Stakem, Patrick H. *The Saturn Rocket and the Pegasus Missions, 1965,* 2013, PRRB Publishing, ISBN-1520209916.

Stakem, Patrick H. *Visiting the NASA Centers, and Locations of Historic Rockets & Spacecraft,* 2017, PRRB Publishing, ISBN-1549651205.

Stakem, Patrick H. *Microprocessors in Space*, 2011, PRRB Publishing, ISBN-1520216343.

Stakem, Patrick H. Computer *Virtualization and the Cloud*, 2013, PRRB Publishing, ISBN-152021636X.

Stakem, Patrick H. *What's the Worst That Could Happen? Bad Assumptions, Ignorance, Failures and Screw-ups in Engineering Projects, 2014,* PRRB Publishing, ISBN-1520207166.

Stakem, Patrick H. *Computer Architecture & Programming of the Intel x86 Family, 2013,* PRRB Publishing, ISBN-1520263724.

Stakem, Patrick H. *The Hardware and Software Architecture of the Transputer*, 2011,PRRB Publishing, ISBN-152020681X.

Stakem, Patrick H. *Mainframes, Computing on Big Iron*, 2015, PRRB Publishing, ISBN- 1520216459.

Stakem, Patrick H. *Spacecraft Control Centers*, 2015, PRRB Publishing, ISBN-1520200617.

Stakem, Patrick H. *Embedded in Space,* 2015, PRRB Publishing, ISBN-1520215916.

Stakem, Patrick H. *A Practitioner's Guide to RISC Microprocessor Architecture*, Wiley-Interscience, 1996, ISBN-0471130184.

Stakem, Patrick H. *Cubesat Engineering*, PRRB Publishing, 2017, ISBN-1520754019.

Stakem, Patrick H. *Cubesat Operations*, PRRB Publishing, 2017, ISBN-152076717X.

Stakem, Patrick H. *Interplanetary Cubesats*, PRRB Publishing, 2017, ISBN-1520766173 .

Stakem, Patrick H. Cubesat Constellations, Clusters, and Swarms, Stakem, PRRB Publishing, 2017, ISBN-1520767544.

Stakem, Patrick H. *Graphics Processing Units, an overview*, 2017, PRRB Publishing, ISBN-1520879695.

Stakem, Patrick H. *Intel Embedded and the Arduino-101, 2017,* PRRB Publishing, ISBN-1520879296.

Stakem, Patrick H. *Orbital Debris, the problem and the mitigation*, 2018, PRRB Publishing, ISBN-*1980466483.*

Stakem, Patrick H. *Manufacturing in Space*, 2018, PRRB Publishing, ISBN-1977076041.

Stakem, Patrick H. *NASA's Ships and Planes*, 2018, PRRB Publishing, ISBN-1977076823.

Stakem, Patrick H. *Space Tourism*, 2018, PRRB Publishing, ISBN-1977073506.

Stakem, Patrick H. *STEM – Data Storage and Communications*, 2018, PRRB Publishing, ISBN-1977073115.

Stakem, Patrick H. *In-Space Robotic Repair and Servicing*, 2018, PRRB Publishing, ISBN-1980478236.

Stakem, Patrick H. *Introducing Weather in the pre-K to 12 Curricula, A Resource Guide for Educators*, 2017, PRRB Publishing, ISBN-1980638241.

Stakem, Patrick H. *Introducing Astronomy in the pre-K to 12 Curricula, A Resource Guide for Educators*, 2017, PRRB Publishing, ISBN-198104065X.
Also available in a Brazilian Portuguese edition, ISBN-1983106127.

Stakem, Patrick H. *Deep Space Gateways, the Moon and Beyond*, 2017, PRRB Publishing, ISBN-1973465701.

Stakem, Patrick H. *Exploration of the Gas Giants, Space Missions to Jupiter, Saturn, Uranus, and Neptune*, PRRB Publishing, 2018, ISBN-9781717814500.

Stakem, Patrick H. *Crewed Spacecraft*, 2017, PRRB Publishing, ISBN-1549992406.

Stakem, Patrick H. *Rocketplanes to Space*, 2017, PRRB Publishing, ISBN-1549992589.

Stakem, Patrick H. *Crewed Space Stations,* 2017, PRRB Publishing, ISBN-1549992228.

Stakem, Patrick H. *Enviro-bots for STEM: Using Robotics in the pre-K to 12 Curricula, A Resource Guide for Educators,* 2017, PRRB Publishing, ISBN-1549656619.

Stakem, Patrick H. *STEM-Sat, Using Cubesats in the pre-K to 12 Curricula, A Resource Guide for Educators*, 2017, ISBN-1549656376.

Stakem, Patrick H. *Lunar Orbital Platform-Gateway*, 2018, PRRB Publishing, ISBN-1980498628.

Stakem, Patrick H. *Embedded GPU's*, 2018, PRRB Publishing, ISBN- 1980476497.

Stakem, Patrick H. *Mobile Cloud Robotics*, 2018, PRRB Publishing, ISBN- 1980488088.

Stakem, Patrick H. *Extreme Environment Embedded Systems,* 2017, PRRB Publishing, ISBN-1520215967.

Stakem, Patrick H. *What's the Worst, Volume-2*, 2018, ISBN-1981005579.

Stakem, Patrick H., *Spaceports*, 2018, ISBN-1981022287.

Stakem, Patrick H., *Space Launch Vehicles*, 2018, ISBN-1983071773.

Stakem, Patrick H. *Mars*, 2018, ISBN-1983116902.

Stakem, Patrick H. *X-86, 40th Anniversary ed*, 2018, ISBN-1983189405.

Stakem, Patrick H. *Lunar Orbital Platform-Gateway*, 2018, PRRB Publishing, ISBN-1980498628.

Stakem, Patrick H. *Space Weather*, 2018, ISBN-1723904023.

Stakem, Patrick H. *STEM-Engineering Process*, 2017, ISBN-1983196517.

Stakem, Patrick H. *Space Telescopes,* 2018, PRRB Publishing, ISBN-1728728568.

Stakem, Patrick H. *Exoplanets*, 2018, PRRB Publishing, ISBN-9781731385055.

Stakem, Patrick H. *Planetary Defense*, 2018, PRRB Publishing, ISBN-9781731001207.

Patrick H. Stakem *Exploration of the Asteroid Belt*, 2018, PRRB Publishing, ISBN-1731049846.

Patrick H. Stakem *Terraforming*, 2018, PRRB Publishing, ISBN-1790308100.

Patrick H. Stakem, *Martian Railroad,* 2019, PRRB Publishing, ISBN-1794488243.

Patrick H. Stakem, *Exoplanets,* 2019, PRRB Publishing, ISBN-1731385056.

Patrick H. Stakem, *Exploiting the Moon,* 2019, PRRB Publishing, ISBN-1091057850.

Patrick H. Stakem, *RISC-V, an Open Source Solution for Space Flight Computers,* 2019, PRRB Publishing, ISBN-1796434388.

Patrick H. Stakem, *Arm in Space*, 2019, PRRB Publishing, ISBN-9781099789137.

Patrick H. Stakem, *Extraterrestrial Life*, 2019, PRRB Publishing, ISBN-978-1072072188.

Patrick H. Stakem, *Space Command*, 2019, PRRB Publishing, ISBN-978-*1693005398*.